Japanese Mythology

A Fascinating Introduction to Japanese Mythology

(Exploring the Ancient Stories, Legends, and Folktales of the Land of the Rising Sun)

Edwin Cruz

Published By **John Kembrey**

Edwin Cruz

All Rights Reserved

Japanese Mythology: A Fascinating Introduction to Japanese Mythology (Exploring the Ancient Stories, Legends, and Folktales of the Land of the Rising Sun)

ISBN   978-0-9938301-7-4

No part of this guidebook shall be reproduced in any form without permission in writing from the publisher except in the case of brief quotations embodied in critical articles or reviews.

Legal & Disclaimer

The information contained in this book is not designed to replace or take the place of any form of medicine or professional medical advice. The information in this book has been provided for educational & entertainment purposes only.

The information contained in this book has been compiled from sources deemed reliable, and it is accurate to the best of the Author's knowledge; however, the Author cannot guarantee its accuracy and validity and cannot be held liable for any errors or omissions. Changes are periodically made to this book. You must consult your doctor or get professional medical advice before using any of the suggested remedies, techniques, or information in this book.

Upon using the information contained in this book, you agree to hold harmless the Author from and against any damages, costs, and expenses, including any legal fees potentially resulting from the application of any of the information provided by this guide. This disclaimer applies to any damages or injury caused by the use and application, whether directly or indirectly, of any advice or information presented, whether for breach of contract, tort, negligence, personal injury, criminal intent, or under any other cause of action.

You agree to accept all risks of using the information presented inside this book. You need to consult a professional medical practitioner in order to ensure you are both able and healthy enough to participate in this program.

Table Of Contents

Chapter 1: The History Of Japanese Mythology.. 1

Chapter 2: Japanese Kamis 21

Chapter 3: Mythology Terminology 47

Chapter 4: Amaterasu And The Cave 56

Chapter 5: The One-Inch Boy – Issun-Boshi 63

Chapter 6: Susanoo And Orochi 72

Chapter 7: The Tongue-Cut Sparrow 82

Chapter 8: The Peach Boy – Momotaro 105

Chapter 9: History Of Japan 116

Chapter 10: The Principles Of Skiing 140

Chapter 11: The Origin Of The World ... 155

Chapter 12: The Divine Origins Of The Emperors 173

Chapter 1: The History Of Japanese Mythology

Japanese mythology is a hard and fast of reminiscences which have been made from oral traditions that have been surpassed down thru the generations that noted the data in their humans, practices, customs, ceremonies, gods, and legends. Japanese mythology has a long records that dates returned over 2000 years. It changed into converted into maximum vital religions. One is an indigenous religion called Shinto. The different end up Buddhism that modified into created in India and changed into added into Japan from Korea and China.

Their mythology consists of many spirits, goddesses, and gods. Most of those memories speak approximately how the arena modified into created, how the islands of Japan were fashioned, and all the sports of the magical creatures, spirits, animals, human beings, and deities. Some were set in places just like the underworld and heaven.

Japanese Myth Sources

Most of these myths that have survived the times had been recorded inside the Nihonshoki and the Kojiki. The Kojiki changed into created for the imperial court docket. It homes the region's creation, how the gods originated, and the Japanese emperors' ancestry. They claim to have descended from Amaterasu, the solar goddess. These books knowledgeable of the ruling elegance's origins and had been used to strengthen their authority. Because of this, these aren't herbal myths but have been coloured through politics. These have been based totally totally on traditions: The Izumo Cycle and the Yamato Cycle. The Izumo Cycle is based totally mostly on the individual of Susanoo no Mikoto, who is Amaterasu's brother. They Yamato Cycle is based totally mostly on Amaterasu Omikami, the solar goddess.

The Nihonshoki have grow to be finished in 720 and contained many legends and myths.

It additionally enables to set up the Imperial own family's family tree. The Nihonshoki turned into endorsed hundreds by the use of Korean and Chinese mythology and facts. Both the Nihonshoki and the Kojiki embody some elements of Taoism. This is a Chinese religion that end up delivered to Japan within the 600s.

Mythological facts and genealogies have been saved from about the 700s and possibly masses longer than that. By Emperor Temmu's time, which modified into within the 800s, it was critical to understand all of the people within the families who have been important so they could establish their positions for each one in the 8 tiers of call and rank that turn out to be created primarily based at the Chinese courtroom tool. Because of this, Temmu ordered them to create books about the genealogies and myths that resulted within the Nihonshoki and Kojiki. The individuals who made the ones and specific files had all the documented and oral sources at their disposal. There had been extra resources available to the those who created the Nihonshoki. Even even though the Kojiki has more myths and circle of relatives tree in it, the Nihonshoki offers greater understandings of each their folklore and the history of early Japan. The primary motive of it changed into to provide the Sinicized court docket a records that they may have a look at with the Chinese annals.

Major Characters and Deities

The motive in the again of growing the Nihonshoki and the Kojiki emerge as to trace the imperial circle of relatives tree all the way lower returned to the appearance of the area. You can find out the Yamato Cycle myths effects in these money owed. At the start of the arena, it became a large mass, a dark ooze that end up full of seeds. Slowly, the best debris emerge as heaven or yang, and the large debris modified into earth or yin.

Deities had been created in each: there have been 3 unmarried deities after which numerous divine couples. The Nihonshoki states that the primary three gods that have been herbal male confirmed up like a reed that associated earth to heaven. A customary basis became created for all of the drifting cosmos, after which sand and dirt collected on top of it. A pole have end up pushed into it, and an inhabitable location become eventually created.

The goddess Izanami and the god Izanagi showed up. They have been ordered by manner of their superiors who lived in heaven to create solid land from the substances drifting in the ocean. They have been advised to stand on a floating bridge within the heavens and stir the sea with a spear. They pulled the spear up to appearance if a few factor had collected on the tip. When the salty water dripped off the prevent, it created the island known as Onogoro. This island grew to emerge as stable immediately. Izanami and Izanagi then got here all the way all of the manner right down to live on this island. They grew to end up around spherical a celestial pillar and met every distinct for the primary time. They discovered every one-of-a-type sexually appealing and began out generating topics. After some failures, they created the 8 islands that makeup Japan.

They then created goddesses and gods of the winds, streams, valleys, mountains, timber, and masses of other of Japan's herbal functions. While Izanami became giving shipping to Kagutsuchi, the fireplace god, she modified into significantly burned. While she became loss of lifestyles, she created more goddesses and gods. These goddesses and gods presided over agriculture, earth, and steel. Other deities got here from her husband's tears.

Izanagi have become filled with anger at losing Izanami that he attacked Kagutsuchi. His blood created the god of thunder and other deities. In his grief, Izanagi went after Izanami to Yomi-tsu Kuni, that could be a international of lack of lifestyles and darkness that is taken into consideration to be the underworld, and pleaded together with her to go back again again with him. She knowledgeable him that she had already eaten meals cooked on Yomi's range and couldn't come yet again. Izanami become hiding inside the shadows in order that Izanagi couldn't see her. She asked him now not to observe her, but Izanagi lit a torch and saw that she end up covered in maggots and had already started to decay, and he fled in terror. This made Iaznami feel humiliated and indignant; she despatched hideous spirits after him and chased him out of the underworld. Once he reached the pinnacle global, he blocked the underworld's front with a massive stone. Izanami threatened Izanagi with the resource of telling him that she would possibly kill 1000 humans every day. He stated that he should father 1500 youngsters for each one thousand she killed. Izanami stayed in Yomi and ruled the dead.

Izanagi lower returned to his world and purified himself of the stench from Yomi via the use of bathing in a flow into. As he grow to be undressing, goddesses and gods seemed from his clothing. While he end up cleaning himself, the water that fell out of his left eye created Amaterasu Omikami, the sun goddess. She have become the Imperial Family's ancestress. She is the amazing-regarded deity. She is answerable for fertility and brings light to the area. She has a shrine at Ise, and it's far the most essential shrine in all of Japan.

Amaterasu has brothers who were usual from water that fell from Izanagi's proper eye and nose. Tsukuyomi no Mikoto, the moon god, grow to be shaped from the water that fell from Izanagi's proper eye, and Susanoo became usual from the water that fell from his nose. Tsukiyomi is the moon god, and Susanoo is a violent and effective god who has been associated with storms. Susanoo has a extra essential characteristic in Japanese mythology as he has seemed in severa large legends, which includes many with Amaterasu. He is also said to be a trickster.

Myths of Amaterasu

One fantasy speaks of the manner Susanoo come to be no longer glad along together with his percent and brought on loads of destruction. He changed into quickly banished to Yomi-tsu Kuni. He asked if he have to visit heaven to visit his sister one more time. Amaterasu grow to be concerned that Susanoo must attempt to take over the sky, so she asked if he may additionally take part in a competition.

He agreed to the opposition that would display their powers. If Susanoo won, he may need to stay heaven bit if he out of location, he may want to ought to bypass again to Yomi.

Amaterasu requested her brother for his sword. She broke this into 3 pieces and chewed on it. When she spits out the factors, all of them end up goddesses. Susanoo took a string of beads that had been everyday like stars that Amaterasu had given to him. He chewed at the beads and spat out five gods. He claimed victory when you consider that he had created five gods, and Amaterasu had most effective created three goddesses. Amaterasu confirmed Susanoo that he had definitely made gods from her possessions; this proved her power become more large than his. Susanoo would in all likelihood now not widely known defeat, and he or she allowed him to live.

Susanoo soon have end up complacent alongside alongside with his success and started out out being a trickster. He did subjects that violated vital taboos and irritated his sister. He flung excrement at some point of Amaterasu's eating room at the same time as she changed into celebrating the number one fruit's ceremony. He destroyed fields of rice, made horribly loud noises, and stored the floors of her palace filthy. Susanoo killed considered one in every of heaven's horses, skinned it, and hurled it into a hall in which she changed into weaving cloth.

Amaterasu modified into enraged together collectively along with his pranks, and he or she hid in a celestial cave and could not come out. When she hid herself, speedy darkness blanketed the earth and heavens. The vegetation stopped growing, and the whole thing got here to a screeching halt. The gods didn't recognize what to do, so 800 of them in the end gathered to talk approximately strategies to get her out of the cave. One god referred to as Omori-Kane came up with a solution. The gods accrued at the entrance to the cave and hung a mirror on a department of a tree that grew outdoor the cave. A more youthful goddess, Amemouzume, no Mikoto, danced half-naked. The gods laughed and applauded loudly. Amaterasu heard the commotion and wondered what changed into happening out of doors the cave. She opened the cave's door a piece and requested why they have been glad. They lied to her and stated they have been celebrating because of the fact they observed a goddess who changed into better than her. She have emerge as curious as to who that would be, and he or she opened the door a bit wider. She found her photo within the mirror. When she paused to examine herself, a god who became hiding close by pulled her out of the cave. Another god blocked the cave's front with a mystical rope. When Amaterasu got here out of the cave, her light started out shining, and existence over again. The gods banished Susanoo from heaven as punishment for all of the problems he had triggered.

The Izumo Cycle

Soon the Izumo Cycle myths commenced out to appear within the memories, and Okuninushi have become the precept individual within the ones myths. Since he had angered the gods of heaven, Susanoo have become banished from heaven. He descended to Izumo, in which he rescued Kishiinada Hime or the Princess Marvellous Rice Field from a serpent with eight heads. He married the princess and have become the forefather of the Izumo, a ruling own family.

The member of his circle of relatives that turn out to be the maximum important become Okuninushi no Mikoto or the amazing earth leader. He controlled this location earlier than the descendants of the sun goddess came to earth.

One of the greater famous tales is set the White Rabbit. This story goes a few aspect like this: Okuninushi had 80 brothers, and they all wanted to marry the equal princess. On one journey to look this princess, the men discovered a rabbit with none fur in quite a few ache beside the road. They tricked the animal via telling it that it may get its coat lower returned thru the usage of bathing in a few saltwater. This in reality made the rabbit's pain worse. Okuninushi came upon the rabbit a bit time later. He asked the rabbit what had befell to him; the rabbit cautioned him the tale of the way he misplaced his fur.

The rabbit have been travelling amongst islands, and he asked a few crocodiles to create a bridge to the rabbit must skip with out getting wet. In go back for this, the rabbit has promised he might rely the crocodiles to see if there were greater of them than all the creatures within the sea. As the rabbit were given toward the shore, the crocodiles discovered out that his promise turn out to be best a trick to get to the possibility shore. The ultimate crocodile had been given mad and grabbed the rabbit and tore off its fur. When Okuninushi heard his tale, he advocated the rabbit to take a tub in clear water after which roll spherical inside the grass pollen that had fallen to the ground. The rabbit did as directed, and new white fur soon began developing on his body. This rabbit changed into a god, and he rewarded Okuninushi with the useful resource of telling him that he want to marry the stunning princess. Okuninishi's success made his brothers irritated, and there are various more myths about all the struggles among them.

A Divine Emperor

It wasn't lengthy in advance than Amaterasu requested Okuninushi to offer her the land of Izumo. She felt like "the land of the big reed-blanketed plains and glowing rice ears" want to be ruled with the aid of her descendants. Once Izumo changed into given to her, she had Ninigi no Mikoto, her grandson, come to earth. It states within the Nihonshoki that Amaterasu gave Ninigi a few rice ears from the sacred rice area and informed him to plant rice on land at the same time as worshipping the celestial gods. She additionally gave him the replicate that have become used to get her out of the cave, alongside component some jewels and the sword that belonged to Susanoo. He then came to earth and landed on Mount Fuji. He married one of the mountain god's daughters, whose call modified into Konohana-Sakuya Hime. With the treasures that he turn out to be sent to earth with, all of us preferred him as Japan's pointers, and people treasures have emerge as the Imperial Family treasures.

Once his associate were given pregnant and grow to be going into labor, multi characteristic night time, he desired evidence that the kid emerge as simply his. She set her room on hearth and gave start to a few sons. One son have end up the father of Jimmu Tenno, the number one emperor. He marked the time in information a number of the chronological age and the "age of the gods." His conquest of the Japanese heartland and eastern day adventure emerge as just a fable.

Hachiman

The maximum well-known deity in Japanese mythology is Hachiman. He have become the client of warriors. Hachiman's individual have emerge as based completely totally on Ohin, the emperor, who lived inside the 300s, and we are identified for his military skills. According to legend, even as Ojin died, he changed into the god Hachiman. He have become part of the Shinto pantheon.

Inari

There is a god called Inari who appears in a number of the myths. He is critical because of the reality he's related to growing rice, this is Japans' primary meals crop. Inari come to be idea to supply them prosperity and is the client of sword makers and buyers.

Spirits and Other Creatures

There are many creatures and spirits in Japanese mythology referred to as the tengu. These are minor deities who're element chicken and detail human. They live inside the mountainous areas and live in timber there. They love playing hints on people however don't like being tricked. They aren't as wicked as they may be mischievous.

One threatening employer of spirits is called the Oni. They originated in China and traveled to Japan with Buddhism. These are horned demons and are typically massive in period. They can address an animal or human form. They are every so often invisible, and they're capable of scouse borrow human souls. They can be merciless and had been related to evil forces like ailment and famine.

This mythology is composed of various deities from Buddhism, too. Other than the reminiscences about Buddha, there are various testimonies approximately Amida, who end up the ruler of Pure Land, which changed into paradise. The protector of girls in childbirth and children was called Kannon. Jizo rescues souls from hell are distinct essential figures in Buddhism.

Major Themes and Myths

The tales which are most critical to Japanese myths deal with the goddess Amaterasu and advent. These are deeply rooted in nature, and they describe in element how the lands had been shaped and the origins of mild, wind, and hearth.

As stated above, inside the Kojiki, there was simply ooze that the earth and heavens long-established out of. Life soon emerged out of this ooze. There were three deities in heaven, and soon more appeared. These five deities have end up the "Separate Heavenly Deities." They have been brief observed thru the "Seven Generations of the Age of the Gods," which had been crafted from five male and woman couples and unmarried deities. The unmarried gods got here from a reed that have come to be floating within the ooze.

Magical Creatures

There is a set of creatures that look like monkeys which can be referred to as the kappa. They show each evil and right developments inside the Japanese myths. They had been associated with water, and that they stay in lakes, ponds, and rivers. They supply water in a hole spot at the pinnacle of their head. If water spills, they lose their magical powers. Kappas drink the blood of livestock, horses, and those. They may also even eat cucumbers. It is said that households may also moreover need to keep away from getting attacked thru them via using throwing cucumbers which have their names on them into their watery homes.

The kappas do have a few actual characteristics as they'll be very well mannered. When they meet everyone, they will bow, which commonly reasons them to spill the water from their heads. They moreover maintain a few component promise they made. In most myths, people can outwit kappa by way of making them make promises.

The Legacy of Japan's Mythology

Mythology nevertheless performs a large characteristic in the lives of the Japanese. Legends and myths are the concept of most of their literature, drama, and paintings. People are even though studying and telling reminiscences approximately those goddesses and gods. Their kagura dances are completed to honor the deities of the Shinto shrine. Legend has traced the starting vicinity of this art shape to the dance that had been given Amaterasu out of her cave.

Chapter 2: Japanese Kamis

Within the Shinto religion, the word kami is a term that could imply supernatural powers, herbal phenomena, ancestors, deified mortals, spirits, and gods. All of those must have an effect on someone's lifestyles each day, and in order that they get worshipped, asked for help, and given offerings. There had been a few cases when they had been even appealed to for their divination shills. Kami receives interested by purity, each the spiritual and the bodily, and that they get repelled by way of the use of way of not sufficient of it, and this consists of any and all disharmony. Kami has been associated with nature and might be gift at locations like surprisingly original rocks, timber, waterfalls, and mountains. Because of this, there are about 8 million kami. Most kami are known at a few stage in the country, but many belong to just a small network. Every family might also have its very own ancestry of kami.

People being reverent to spirits that stay in locations of beauty, character animals, and meteorological phenomena date again to about the primary millennium BCE. If you upload all of those to the Shinto gods, circle of relatives ancestors, and heroes collectively with the bodhisattvas that came from Buddhism and you have a countless variety of kami. There is one factor this isn't uncommon with all kami are the four natures or spirits. One of those might be stronger relying on the occasions: sakimitama manner nurturing, kushimatama manner wonderous, nigimitama way lifestyles- helping or mild, and aramitama or hard or wild. These divisions display that kami are able to both evil and superb. In spite of their big numbers, kami can be positioned into different classes. There are diverse strategies to these categorizations. Some students will use kami's characteristic at the same time as others use their nature. To make it less difficult, because those cited normally overlap masses.

Classical Kami

Classical kami are those that seem in the oldest texts much like the Nihonshoki and the Kojiki. In this, you may find out the gods. The maximum amazing among them is Amaterasu. Others will include her brother Susanoo, Okuninushi, Takamimusubi, and the gods of introduction Izanagi and Izanami. The gods who stayed inside the heavens are typically called amatsukami or heavenly kami.

In comparison, the subsequent generation of gods ruled on earth first is known as kunitsukami or earthly kami. All kami in instances of disaster will gather for a convention on the Heavenly River dried riverbed. Most important rocks, caves, mountains, and rivers can also have their very own kami. There are also kami who come from across the ocean, and they're Sarutahiko and Kukunabikona.

Later Kami

The subsequent organization of kami is the ones who had been diagnosed after the early works have been written. This isn't announcing that they weren't worshipped at a preceding time. In this employer, we've Hachiman. He changed into the god of subculture and war. Inari, who become the exchange and rice god, is likewise on this group. The Japanese Emperor, who is reigning, is likewise taken into consideration to be a residing kami. Any phenomena like wind, rain, and sunshine might be kami. The most well-known is the divine wind or kamikaze that blew in opposition to the Mongol fleet that became invading Japan at some degree within the 13th century CE. Some human beings had been worshipped after their demise. Some of these are former emperors, Tenman Tenjin, and the founding father of the Tokugawa shogunal dynasty, Tokugawa Ieyasu. Some foreign places gods were established as kami. The maximum exquisite are Indra and Brahma, the Hindu gods, and Kannon, the Buddhist god. There also are "Seven Lucky Gods" or the schichifukujin: Jurojin, Hotei, Fukurokuju, Ebisu, Daikoku, Bishamon, and Benten. These are a mixed institution of Japanese, Buddhist, Hindu, and Chinese gods, and they are a outstanding example of the way Shinto has converted, absorbed, and welcomed foreign places deities into their massive pantheon of kami.

Local Kami

The next institution is the community kami. Even notwithstanding the truth that plenty of those are giant sorts that have been recognized as effective all through Japan, there is Ryujin or dragon kami, who is the kami of limitations and crossroads. There also are kami of individual families, villages, and prominent close by natural talents. There might be times at the same time as white animals are given a kami. Most close by kami will seem in pairs an excellent manner to typically be one female and one male.

Worshipping Kami

Kami is appeased, nourished, and appealed to try and make certain their have an effect on is and could stay exquisite. Offerings like prayers, vegetation, ingredients, and rice wine might also need to help you obtain this purpose.

Music, dancing, rituals, and fairs can do this too. Shrines from large complexes to easy affairs had been constructed to honor them. Each twelve months, the item or picture that is perception to be a physical manifestation of the kami receives taken thru the community to purify it and to make certain of its well-being. The kami which have end up concept to be embodied via a herbal feature modified into Mount Fuji. This is the first-rate instance and gets visited by using the use of the usage of worshippers as a manner to pay homage.

Kami in preference to God

If the English phrase "god" receives translated into Japanese, it's also represented with the useful resource of the kanji man or woman and is stated kami. To no longer misunderstand, it'd be super to consider "god," "kanji," and "kami" as 3 separate things.

"God" is normally the great omnipresent being that gets capitalized to expose the deity has a completely unique nature that draws a difference with all of the special gods of all of the distinct religions.

Japan's kami became to start with idea to be anthropomorphized herbal phenomena. These encompass any of the kami which may be in the Kojiki and the Nihonshoki, something that possesses notable traits like the sea, rain, wind, moon, and sun, together with the kami which can be worshipped at shrines. Other kami may also consist of human beings, animals, small plant life, wooden, and huge rocks. This is how they have been given described in some unspecified time inside the destiny of the 18th century thru the Japanese college students of the Motoori Norinaga. According to this, a few aspect that inspired sensitivity and awe to a fleeting splendor could be a kami.

For the Japanese folks who acquire as proper with on this, their the us is a land complete of herbal landscapes wherein kami may be decided anywhere you switch. Basically, it's far a kami no Kuni or u.S.A. Of the usa of kami. If you have been to translate this phrase into English, it'd be called "God's u . S . A .." It could be with out issue misunderstood as a "fanatically nationalistic expression," but this isn't what this word manner.

Blended Faith

Japan's religion that is based absolutely mostly on worshipping kami is known as

Shinto. There aren't any statistics that show what life became like sooner or later of historic instances, and most of these information aren't smooth. We can't say if there have been any rituals or ideals that could be called Shinto.

It is possible that this religion came about as a mixture of severa factors, which encompass:

Worshipping of own family gods after which building shrines through the use of manner of the community organizations and groups

The effect of funeral rituals and gala's from Chinese thinkings, calendar research, astronomy, and divination that are associated with the mythical figures which can be known as "divine immortals."

The bronze mirrors and guns that have been added from China and used in magic rituals and festivals with the resource of the use of their chiefs

Worshipping clay collectible collectible figurines as the image for crop fertility and all the shamanism that have come to be added from the Yayoi Period inside the Korean Peninsula as fast as rice farming have turn out to be regular

Hunter-gatherers worshipped nature in the course of the Jomon duration

The Japanese started out thinking about those elements together as "Shinto" whilst Buddhism got here into Japan. They then in contrast this new faith with their ordinary practices.

Buddhas and Kami

Buddhism come to be formed in India with the aid of using Gautama Buddha. He become born in every the fifth or sixth century BC. There had been many tales written about Buddha that consists of a complex set of doctrines. Before it came to Japan, it changed into changed on its journey in the path of China, wherein all of the numerous texts were translated, and non secular orders had been prepared and completed in Chinese style. The

Japanese evolved their kami with the useful resource of contrasting them with the Buddhas. The important versions are:

Buddhists create statues and likenesses of Buddhas and put them in temples, but the Buddha doesn't stay in the ones temples. Believers of Shinto don't make likenesses of kami. Objects to attract kami are known as yorishiro. They get placed on shrines, but kami don't stay in these shrines.

Buddhas are typically men, but they received't ever marry. Kami may additionally moreover need to each be lady or male, and they'll on occasion get married.

Buddhas are living humans who've reached the most remarkable enlightenment. When a Buddha dies, they've got sooner or later escaped from the cycle of loss of life and lifestyles, and that they not exist. Kami is extremely good than everyday humans. Some kami are ancestors of humans and will each die or stay.

Along with different types of superior Chinese lifestyle similar to the ritsuryo machine of shape, treatment, calendar research, astronomy, and centralized government, Buddha become a tool that the ruling beauty used to stable its repute and energy. After introducing those new beliefs, Shinto and Buddhism started out occupying special areas in the Japanese faith.

The Appeal of Buddhism and the Reform of Shinto

The Yamato Court began about the third century AD in what is now referred to as the Kansai place. This modified proper into a confederation of all of the forces in the path of the region. They believed the fine prolonged own family who had been certified to carry out rituals were the descendants of Amaterasu. The humans in special regions regarded to severa ancestors much like the those who lived in Izumo worshipped Okuninushi. Myths approximately the harmonious existence of the severa kami supported forming a confederation.

During the eighth century, the Kojiki and the Nihonshoki were finished. These compilations about the records and legends placed Amaterasu because the most influential kami, and all of the emperors were her descendants. These are the quality those who can inherit the right to do rituals. Because of this, any forces out of doors of the imperial line out of place all of these rights. The Yamato government didn't study it this manner and installation a "one god" faith just like the humans of Israel did after they declared Yahweh to be the best right God. Rather, and this gave them the positions of hierarchy that became beneath Amaterasu. She has the cooperation among all the other kami, and this strengthened the collaboration amongst various corporations.

By searching at it this manner, Buddhas had been extraordinary due to the truth they have been in reality separated from the kami. This way they didn't should be subordinate to Amaterasu. Anyone who were excluded from the emperor's monopoly approximately strength and formality after the reform of Shinto want to adopt Buddhism within the occasion that they decided on to perform that. All of those forces had been located spherical and in Yamato Province, it's miles now Nara Prefecture. By inheriting a bureaucratic authorities, that that that they had superior into an aristocracy. Many of them embraced Buddhism. They built temples and was hoping to be born another time in the Western Paradise. The idea of being reincarnated as a Buddha after one died emerge as very special from the Shinto tenets. In comparison, any of the peasants who labored at any of the estates that belonged to the aristocracy, shrines, and temples, their faith in close by kami became more herbal and acquainted than Buddhism.

Various Ideas approximately Death and Life

How did the Japanese view the afterworld? Well, a few idea that their soul may return to the mountain. Others believed that they might pass underground to the land of lack of life called Yoni. While others thought they may go with the flow the sea proper right into a paradise that was referred to as Tokoyo. Some human beings believed in defilement that become related to loss of life, and the vain traveled far from in which dwelling human beings lived.

Every Emperor worshipped Amaterasu, other kami, and their private ancestors. All the non secular ceremonies were primarily based mostly on the Chinese fashions however honoring their deceased ancestors grow to be first-class located in Japan. It became idea that the dead emperors grow to be kami after their defilement were cleansed in somewhere that changed into very far away.

In assessment, Buddhism says that humans ought to paintings to acquire nirvana thru doing ascetic practices whilst going through the cycle of existence and into dying. If a person died without mission nirvana, they had been right away reincarnated into new our bodies to begin their lives time and again. They didn't consider inside the land of the useless, and those didn't have an everlasting soul. Basically, particular Shinto and Buddhism have truly unique thoughts about loss of life.

The concept of reincarnation wasn't proper away conventional in Japan at the same time as Buddhism become introduced into their u.S.A. Of the us. The Chinese perception that useless humans trade into demons that lived in hell came into Japan through Taoism, and Buddhism started out spreading slowly. Buddhism had been given extra well-known whilst it changed its perspectives to the ones who've been popular through the human beings of Japan.

Meet the Gods

The following kami come from every the Japanese Buddhist and Shinto traditions.

Most had been stimulated with the aid of the use of the usage of Chinese, Indian, Roman, and Greek goddesses and gods.

Jizo

This is the discern of childbirth and youngsters.

The historic Japanese idea that youngsters who died in advance than their parents couldn't move the Sanzu River into the afterlife considering the fact that they hadn't lived prolonged enough to build up enough proper deeds. They have been doomed to stand on the shore of the river and stack small rocks.

The god Jizo permits those kids circulate the river. He does this via hiding them in his gown. Any statue you observe of Jizo can be pretty small. They usually seem in large numbers at temples sooner or later of Japan. There are over 1,000,000 Jizo statues in this u . S . A .. These are usually donated by the dad and mom of lifeless children. Jizo is given hats and bibs to maintain them warm. There can be a few temples in which you could locate stacks of rocks or toys in the front of the Jizo to make certain their infant is stable in the course of their afterlife.

Fujin and Raijin

Fujin is the wind kami who is generally shown preserving a bag complete of wind. Raijin is the typhoon, thunder, and lightning kami. They are normally shown preserving a hammer and surrounded by way of drums.

Fujin and Raijin commonly appear collectively. They are feared hundreds due to the harm that storms and typhoons have wreaked in Japan.

Parents would possibly tell their kids to ensure their bellybutton had been hidden for the duration of a storm simply so Raijin might devour their bellies.

Since those are feared deities, Fuijin and Raijin typically appear collectively on the gate to a shrine to guard it. Every traveler to the ones sacred locations had to pass by way of manner of the usage of the gaze of those deities who have been so horrifying.

Ungaro and Agyo

Ungaro and Agyo are the Buddha's frightening guardians who usually stand at the entrance to any temple in Japan.

Agyo is their symbol of violence. His statues display him baring his teeth and every him clenching his fists or shielding guns. Ungaro stands for power. His mouth will constantly be close, and he indicates that his hands are empty as a sign of self warranty.

Inari

She is the goddess of all the matters which are vital to the Japanese lifestyle like worldly fulfillment, sake, fertility, tea, and rice. Her earthly messengers are foxes. Because of this, foxes preserve a whole lot of recognize in Japan.

Most shrines in Japan may additionally have small shrines to the aspect which have been devoted to foxes. It isn't always unusual to present the foxes an offering of aburaage. It is idea that foxes are loopy about this meals. Most shrines may want to have some statues of foxes at them too.

Kannon

She is the Buddhist goddess of mercy. She is considered to be a Bodhisattva or a person who has carried out enlightenment. She postponed her Buddhahood until absolutely honestly all people has been enlightened.

Most temples were devoted to worship her. She is also featured within the Japanese Christian imagery of the Edo-generation.

During the 1600s, Japan banned Christianity. The Christians still worshiped in secrecy. These Christians made statues to honor Kannon that regarded loads similar to the Roman Catholic's Madonna and Child. They covered a few Christian symbols like crosses.

Some figures have survived for many years and may be seen at some Japanese temples however these days.

Benzaiten

This goddess is also referred to as Benten. She is the goddess of the whole thing that flows like track, eloquence, and terms. She has moreover been associated with love. It isn't uncommon for any shrine that has been committed to her to be idea of as a romantic spot for couples. She is one of the Seven Lucky Gods.

The Enoshima Shrine that modified into dedicated to Benzaiten may be very famous with couples because of its red prayer boards with hearts.

Ebisu or Yebisu

Yebisu is now and again written as Ebisu. He turn out to be born without bones and struggled just to stay. When he was two, he grow to be located into the ocean in a boat. He did stay on, and he grew bones. He came again from the ocean severa years later to be considered as a god.

He is the god of achievement, fishermen, and he guards small kids and the fireside. He is extremely joyful in spite of the reality that he has had a difficult life.

Yebisu is commonly seen as a obese man carrying a hat and carrying a fishing rod with a fish. In more cutting-edge instances, he has been called the god at the Yebisu beer cans.

Amaterasu

She is the goddess of the universe and sun. She has been considered as the most essential Shinto god. The Emperor is perception to be a descendant of Amaterasu. This modified into emphasised at a few diploma in the years between 1868 to 1945 on the equal time as Shinto become a government enterprise employer. When WWII end up over, Emperor Showa made a statement over the radio that he did no longer recall himself as a kami.

Shitenno

This translates to "Four Heavenly Kings." These are four gods who are terrifying and have been borrowed from the Hindu to guard the Buddhist temples. Every god is associated with a selected detail, unique function, season, or path. In most instances, Shitenno is confirmed stomping on demons.

Izanagi and Izanami

Izanami and Izanagi are the Shinto gods of introduction. The created the earth via the use of manner of the usage of a spear that were embellished with jewels. They used this spear to stir the ocean located most of the earth and heaven. Every time a drop of water fell off the spear, it created an island.

Tengu

This is a fowl monster that would take at the form of a human. When they are in human shape, they'll have huge noses.

Tengu has constantly been idea of due to the fact the enemy of Buddhism who corrupted monks and their lovers. In modern times, they had been considered because the protectors of sacred mountains and forests.

Tengu isn't commonly kami. They are normally taken into consideration to be ghosts or monsters. But, a few temples that are placed in sacred mountains and forests have been related to tengu kami.

Sugawara no Michizane

This kami become a incredible Japanese politician and poet who were given exiled through his warring parties in 901. He died a lonely man quick after this.

Immediately after he died, Kyoto modified into struck with hundreds of floods and terrible lightning. All of the sons of the Emperor died in uncommon injuries. Droughts and plague unfold wildly through Japan.

The government said this have come to be due to Sugawara no Michizane's vengeful spirit. They restored his fame and ranked posthumously. They tried to remove all of the proof of his punishment. When the catastrophe endured happening, they gave his spirit the turn out to be privy to of Kami of Scholarship for unique ceremonies. They built a shrine in Kyoto to honor him. It is referred to as the Kitano Tenmangu Shrine. The failures ultimately ended.

Taira no Masakado

He become a samurai that challenged the Imperial court docket located in Kyoto. He took over large parts of Japan in advance than he changed into defeated in conflict in the 12 months 940. They brought his head again to Tokyo, and he changed into enshrined at Kanda Shrine.

Taira no Masakado modified into very famous with the humans for the motive that he challenged the authorities. There had been rainbows, lunar eclipses, butterfly swarms, and earthquakes in Kyoto before his rebellion.

He modified into taken into consideration to be a completely powerful kami. He needs to be appeased continuously, or lousy luck will occur. He has been blamed for fires and floods within the Edo-generation. The Shoguns may go to his shrine to preference for him.

Chapter 3: Mythology Terminology

Since the unique testimonies were written in Japanese, a few terminology can be a piece difficult to recognize if you aren't familiar with the Japanese language. On a similar be conscious, their symbolism may be a bit exclusive than what a few are used to as well. To ensure you recognize and recognize the memories, we're capable of skip over some terms and symbolism that you may locate useful.

Glossary

Aku – manner evil, however the which means that does not best embody moral evil, but moreover includes disappointment, misfortune, and inferiority.

Anzen – it's far a shape of omamori, specially for protection. Its number one motive is protection at artwork and is frequently requested from a kami.

Aramitama – approach wild soul, and refers back to the violent and hard issue of a entire spirit.

Bon Matsuri – a opposition this is held spherical July fifteenth to assist console the spirits of loss of existence. This is, in principle, a Buddhist competition. In workout, despite the fact that, it is a own family and ancestor festival part of Shinto.

Bunrei – the division method for a kami in which it produces copies of the unique.

Chi – technique intelligence, information, and records. It is one of the seven virtues.

Chochin – those are paper lanterns which may be gift at Shinto gala's.

Chugi – technique loyalty and duty. It is one of the seven virtues.

Daijosai – that may be a ceremony that marks the start of an Emperor's reign.

Dosojin – a group of kami that protects locations of transition, roads, and borders.

Gi – way righteousness. It is one of the seven virtues.

Giri – method burden, responsibility, duty, and duty. It is one of the seven virtues.

Goryo – an irritated soul this is upset for having died sad or violently.

Haku – way vitalism, soul, and existence stress. It comes from Daoism and is part of the soul this is indissolubly attached to the body and could cross back to the earth after the person dies.

Jin – technique compassion and benevolence. It is one of the seven virtues.

Jisei – approach self-restraint, temperance, and power of thoughts. It is one of the seven virtues.

Kagura – manner divine enjoyment. It is also a type of Shinto dance this is linked to the Emperor and his family. It is also a dance performed at shrines inside the direction of their spiritual rites.

Kakuriyo – it's literal which means is a hidden international, because of this either the spirits or kami or the arena of the useless.

Kami – a term that significantly method deity or spirit, however furthermore has many one-of-a-kind meanings:

Deities pointed out in Japanese mythology and nearby gods who protect families, areas, and villages.

Non-anthropomorphic spirits who're unnamed and are placed in natural phenomena.

A number one enjoy of sacred power.

The well-known definition with the resource of Motoori Norinaga, "a kami is some issue or phenomenon that produces the emotions of worry and awe, without a difference among properly and evil."

Kanjo – the method wherein a kami is transferred to a shrine.

Ko – method filial piety. It is one of the seven virtues.

Kon – way vitalism, soul, and life pressure. It comes from Daoism and is the a part of the soul which can go away the frame and go to heaven as quickly as a person dies. It consists of with it the advent of a physical shape.

Kotodama – that is the supernatural electricity that terms private.

Makoto – manner sincerity and honesty. It is one of the seven virtues.

Meiyo – way honor. It is one of the seven virtues.

Mitama – that is the soul of a dull character or the spirit of a kami.

Onryo – approach vengeful spirit. It is a sort of vengeful spirit; a poltergeist.

Rei – technique etiquette, manners, and admire. It is one of the seven virtues.

Shintai – approach a divine frame. It is a sacred object, normally a sword, jewel, or replicate representing the kami for worship.

Tei – way fraternity. It is one of the seven virtues.

Torii – method chicken perch. It is an iconic Shinto gate this is placed at the entrance of scared areas.

Toro – method a stone lamp case. It is a lantern place in a shrine or temple.

Ujigami – way prolonged family deity. It is a father or mother spirit or god of a specific region in the Shinto area.

Yu – manner braveness. It is one of the seven virtues.

Yurei – manner dark spirit. It is a shape of phantom or ghost.

Symbolism

The Blue Lotus — This is a photograph of understanding and victory for the spirit over the senses. The lotus symbolizes enlightenment and purity, and in each Buddhist lifestyle, the deities are most usually depicted popularity or sitting atop a lotus or keeping one. While the flower is cute, it is best able to be grown in the dust at the bottom of a pond. The Buddhist deities are enlightened beings who have grown out of the dust of the material global. An open blossom is consultant of the possibility of common salvation for sentient beings.

Mirror — The reflect brings forth intelligence to disencumber the mind. It shows the lesson that lifestyles is honestly an phantasm, for a replicate does now not show us the reality. It is handiest a reflected picture of our existence. This makes the reflect a metaphor for the unenlightened mind this is involved with mere appearances.

Bonsai Tree — The monks who delivered the bonsai to Japan noticed the ones timber as symbols for concord a few of the soul, nature, and man. The tree additionally adjustments. The ugly and bizarre shapes of fierce dragons and serpents were lengthy past. Life of their vicinity come to be stability, concord, and peace. The bonsai tree then have come to be a illustration of all that turned into correct.

Koi Fish — The koi fish represents success or correct fortune, but they'll be additionally related to perseverance in adversity and the energy of motive. It represents braveness in Buddhism. Today, those fish are visible due to the fact the development of spirituality and materials.

Butterflies — The butterfly represents the soul of the residing and useless. They are seen as symbols of durability and pride.

Cranes — This chook moreover represents proper fortune and durability. They are carefully associated with the Japanese New Year, further to marriage ceremony ceremonies. They will regularly be woven into a wedding obi or kimono.

Chapter 4: Amaterasu And The Cave

"There are quite some stories available approximately the sun taking a holiday for one cause or every different, and they now not regularly prevent well for every body. The solar is essential for us human beings, as we want it to stay. When it entails a decision to take a bit revel in, human beings regularly item because we may die. But this is wherein we find out ourselves with the story of Amaterasu.

Amaterasu come to be the oldest daughter of Izanagi and Izanami, the creators of Earth. The pair had labored collectively to shape every piece of land on Earth, from the mountains that rose immoderate into the sky to the waters that rippled across the land. After that that they had fashioned the Earth, Izanagi and Izanami favored to form a lifestyles that would folic upon their introduction. They then gave transport to Amaterasu, who's splendor and radiance delivered pleasure to her dad and mom. They located her immoderate in the sky in which simply absolutely everyone may want to see, and she or he blanketed the day in the form of the solar.

Soon after, Amaterasu had two siblings. The god of the moon, Tsuki-Yomi, who changed into very composed and peaceful and grow to be simplest a fragment as colourful as Amaterasu. The god of the seas, Susanoo, who come to be a boy with a horrible temperament who modified into very vulnerable to violent movement. Susanoo's rage and love of inflicting problems within the ocean in the long run introduced on him to be demoted as the god of the underworld, however that could be a exquisite tale for a few different day.

As you may suspect, Susanoo became no longer satisfied about having to be within the underworld. One day, as he modified into taking in some of Amaterasu's rays and taking a harm from the underworld, he gets an idea. He approached Amaterasu with a proposition. Amaterasu become a piece reluctant, given Sunsanoo's mood. She relented and listened to his proposition. He endorsed that they play a game of God making, but they didn't make their rule clears. At the stop of the game, they have got efficiently original eight new Gods, and that they both declared themselves a winner. As Susanoo were given more enraged, Amaterasu left him to loosen up off.

She headed to her weaving room to paintings on a assignment. As Amaterasu was weaving on her loom, there got here an offensive assault from her brother. Infuriated by way of way of manner of how favored and great she have become, Susanoo killed her mare and tossed it into the weaving room. It ruined all the looms and the venture she was running on. It's believed that Susanoo's rage became so exquisite that he killed an attendant girl inside the room or maybe attacked Amaterasu, which delivered approximately the moderate goddess to interrupt out from her palace.

Amaterasu sought shelter in a collapse a mountain, refusing to polish any light or delight upon the sector. The longer she hid within the cave, the Earth commenced out to wither and die. This delivered about demons to begin crawling out of the underworld and wreaking their personal chaos upon the animals, humans, and flowers on the ground of the Earth.

Knowing that the world become not looking so correct, the Gods and Goddesses came together outside of the cave and attempted to entice Amaterasu out of the cave to shine her slight on the Earth all all over again. The

Gods and Goddesses didn't do an amazing way at developing with a plan to get her out.

Their first strive modified into to place a group of roosters out of doors of the cave. They hoped that if Amaterasu heard all of their crowings, she would likely think that it became time for the sun to upward thrust and come out. As you could assume, this plan didn't work so well.

Then they got here up with a plan the usage of a reflect. They placed a huge mirror dealing with into the cave Amaterasu come to be in and leaned it in opposition to a close-by rock. They hung jewels from the timber and commenced out to dance round, urging all the one-of-a-kind Gods and Goddesses to join in. They had was hoping that their festivities may intrigue the solar Goddess so much that she couldn't help however ask what have become taking place. To which they might reply with, 'We have decided a present day lots higher sun goddess!'

They might then reason Amaterasu to appearance outside of the cave and note what all of the commotions had been about. When she did, Amaterasu noticed her personal reflected image in the replicate. She changed into hypnotized through her very very own splendor, inflicting her to move away the cave.

Alas, this did now not education consultation as deliberate. That's whilst the Goddess Uzume came ahead. She is the Goddess of the humanities, revelry, meditation, delight, and sunrise. She recommended that the extraordinary way to get Amaterasu out of her cave is probably with dance. Since she is Goddess of partying and amusing, she had no hassle with doing a dance for Amaterasu, if it technique that it may shop the arena.

The dancing were given Amaterasu's interest, and she or he or he peeked her head out of the cave. When she did this, she noticed the roosters, the reflect, and the enthusiastic dancing goddess. She surely left the cave this time. It become honestly Uzume, but all three subjects strolling collectively to draw her out and distract her from her anger. After she stepped again outdoor, a huge rock have become positioned within the front of the cave to prevent her from hiding away once more. She soon located herself immersed in the leisure of her circle of relatives and pals.

Unable to live dissatisfied and frowning about her misfortune, Amaterasu permit her slight shine upon the Earth another time. As soon as the sector modified into filled with her moderate all yet again, the illness and demons set upon the land receded into the Underworld. Susanoo receives banished from the heavens for causing this problem. He would wander the Earth for awhile having adventures till he in the long run he can get lower back into the pleasant graces of Amaterasu with the resource of giving her the legendary sword, Grass-Cutter."

Chapter 5: The One-Inch Boy – Issun-Boshi

"A long time in the past in a Japanese village, there lived an vintage guy and his partner, who extra than anything, wanted to have a little one. They continuously hoped and needed for the kid. They may additionally want to go to the temple and pray to the gods. 'May we be blessed with a baby,' they could say, 'regardless of the fact that he isn't any large than our thumbs.'

One day, they in the long run had been given the answer to their prayers. Outside their domestic, they will pay interest toddler cries. The vintage couple checked out each distinct and said, 'Perhaps the brilliant Buddha has replied our prayer at final.' He eased the door open and resting on the step become a tiny child. The infant come to be quite adorable, and he become little. They named the boy Issun Boshi, which meant One-Inch Boy, for he wasn't any taller than his father's thumb.

While Issun Boshi in no way grew any bigger, he did develop as tons as be beneficial, healthy, and smart. He had the coronary coronary heart of a lion, and at the equal time as his discern's small lawn have been a normal supply of journey for the small boy, his incredible ambition grow to be to end up a Samurai and serve a Lord in Kyoto. When Issun Boshi turned 12 years vintage, he went to his mother and father and stated, 'Father and Mother, please deliver me your permission to visit the capital city, for I need to peer the arena, examine many things, and make a call for myself.'

His parents had been distraught and scared once they notion about all the lousy subjects that could seem to Issun Boshi is this type of massive metropolis, but further they knew that their boy modified into strong and clever, so they stated that he need to pass. They created a tiny sword for him using a stitching needle. They additionally gave him a rice bowl that he may additionally want to apply as a ship and some chopsticks to use as oars.

As he floated down the river in his rice bowl boat, he used the chopsticks as his paddles whenever the water have turn out to be hard, and he should use his sword to seize fish. After some days, he made it to the city of Kyoto. 'My, what a hectic city this is!' he idea to himself. 'So many people crammed into one vicinity!' He cautiously walked through the streets and dodged cartwheels and feet. He persevered to walk until he got here to a lovely. It became the most essential house within the city. At the lowest of the stairs sat a couple of vibrant black geta, or wooden footwear. They had been the proprietors of the residence, who became the wealthiest lord within the metropolis. This come to be the house of the famous Lord Sanjo.

The door to the huge house opened. Out walked a person who placed on the awesome black shoes that Issun Boshi has visible. The little boy known as out, 'Hello! Hello up there!' The man fast regarded down and around, and even as he noticed no individual, he commenced out to go decrease lower again inner. Issun Boshi known as out yet again, 'Down right proper here! I'm down right here, near your footwear! Please be cautious you don't step on me.' The man, who changed into the lord of the house, bent down and have emerge as surprised to find out the small boy. Issun Boshi bowed and with politeness introduced himself. 'My call,' he commenced, 'is Issun Boshi. I simply have surely arrived in the city, and I would love to be just proper for you.'

The lord picked up the small boy and sat him within the palm of his hand. In a nice voice, the individual requested, 'But what can a fellow which includes you do?'

Issun Boshi had found a hint fly humming across the pinnacle of the lord and problem him. Issun Boshi draws out his makeshift sword and, with a short swat, away went the fly.

'You are quite an wonderful little fellow,' laughed the lord. 'Come, you could artwork for me and stay in my residence.'

And so, tiny Issun Boshi went to live in a huge, cute residence and served the noble lord. He rapid have become pals with anybody that lived there, in particular the princess, the daughter of the lord. It seemed as despite the fact that she grow to be continually via the use of his issue, helping her in a few trouble way he changed into capable of. This could be keeping down the paper she modified into writing on, or simplest by way of the use of on her shoulder and retaining her enterprise organisation whilst she walked thru the gardens of the stunning house. After some time, the princess began out to shape sturdy affection for her little helper.

During the spring, Issun Boshi traveled with the princess and her companion to visit the cherry blossom opposition. While they're visiting lower lower back domestic, they start to concentrate some unusual noises in the lower back of them on the narrow street. They could not see now not a few factor within the shadows on the identical time as all of sudden, a big monster leaped into their path.

Everybody within the institution ran and screamed, that is, absolutely everyone except for Issun Boshi and the princess.

'Who are you, and what do you need?' screamed Issun Boshi.

'I am an oni,' growled the monster.

An oni! The oni have become very horrible creatures, who desired to problem and torment the townspeople. But Issun Boshi advanced and shouted all over again, saying,

'Get out of the manner, you demon! I am right here to protect the princess. Step once more!'

'Ha! We'll see about that!'growled the oni. He snatched up Issun Boshi. 'You are not any larger than a mouse, and a small one at that.' The oni popped him in his mouth, and with a single gulp, he swallowed him complete. Down, down, down, Issun Boshi slid till he plopped into the oni's stomach.

'This oni need to be greater cautious approximately what he eats,' stated Issun Boshi. He pulled out his makeshift sword and started tickling the oni's stomach.

'Ow! Ooh! Agh!' shouted the oni. Shortly, the oni gave out a noisy burp, and out got here Issun Boshi. The oni ran away, burping the whole way.

Issun Boshi raced decrease once more over to the princess. She bent down and picked something up off of the floor. With lots pride, she stated, 'Look, Issun Boshi, the oni have become so scared he dropped his magic hammer. If you're making a preference on it, it'll come proper.'

Issun Boshi bowed to the princess and answered, 'My lady, I have to ask which you make a need.'

'No, Issun Boshi,' stated the princess, 'You gained this because of your bravery. You want to be the number one one to preference on it.'

With that, Issun Boshi took the hammer and said, 'I have already got my outstanding desire, it's to serve you, however if I need to have every extraordinary want, I might want to be as tall as specific people.'

He then exceeded the hammer to the princess, who made a silent desire on it herself. Then and there, Issun Boshi felt himself begin to extend taller. He persisted to develop till he stood beside the princess, a good-looking younger guy.

That night time time, after the princess informed her father about how brave Issun Boshi had been, and he had risked himself to preserve her, the lord have become so happy that he allowed Issun Boshi to marry the princess. With that, the princess's need got here real, too.

Issun Boshi's courageous deeds had been celebrated at some point of the land. He and the princess may stay fortuitously together, collectively with Issun Boshi's proud and glad parents, whom Issun Boshi delivered to the lord's residence to sign up for his new family. From that day on, he have come to be referred to as General Horikawa, a good-looking and gallant Samurai."

Chapter 6: Susanoo And Orochi

"Poor Susanoo. There was no character inside the heavens who appreciated him because of all of the problems he added about. Nobody even desired to be near him. But modified into it in fact his fault that, because the tempest God, he became continuously observed through a flurry of stormy destruction irrespective of wherein he went? Was it honestly his fault that his call meant impetuous men? Which turned into a end up privy to that modified into not so smooth to heat as tons as or perhaps respect?

And then there has been that whole incident with the horse. Susanoo clearly didn't have a clue as to why his high-priced sister had been given so upset. It turn out to be no longer anything greater than a chunk of rowdy a laugh among siblings.

But no man or woman discovered subjects the same way that he did, as traditional. Everybody, he felt, have turn out to be normally overreacting. As his luxurious sister emerged out of the cava, Susanoo modified into banished from the heavens. Before he changed into banished, he acquired silkworms, soybeans, azuki, wheat, millet, and rice. In a quite foul temper, as would be expected, he wandered the province of Izumo, doing his superb not to motive too many issues for the nearby ecology with the typhoon clouds which have been nonetheless following him.

He reached a river while he decided a pair of chopsticks floating downstream. With that, he selected to adventure upstream in hopes of finding a few neighborhood residents.

It wasn't lengthy in advance than his wandering introduced him before an elderly couple who had been crying within the desolate tract. After a touch little little bit of convincing, the 2 aged ones knowledgeable Susanoo, amongst sobs, that seven in their 8 daughters had been eaten with the useful useful resource of a large 8-headed snake called Yamata-no-Orochi. Orochi came every three hundred and sixty five days and can devour one in every of their daughters. They bemoaned that their closing daughter may also quickly befall the same grisly future.

They defined the dragon as having blazing bloodshot eyes, 8 tails, and 8 heads connected to a significant frame that spanned during 8 mounts and 8 valleys. On the again of the dragon grew moss, cypresses, and birches. His underbelly changed into infected and oozed blood and pus.

'I ought to help you out, you understand,' Susanoo casually said after the couple had completed with their story. 'I am the God of Storms, however the whole thing. Even a 100-headed serpent wouldn't be a in shape for me. However, in order for me that will help you, you have to promise me a reward. Let's say, your last daughter? If I kill the snake, I get to hold her as my associate.'

'You're joking,' the elderly guy gasped in horror. 'You're genuinely someone who walked out of the woodland claiming to be a god. You assume us available over our remaining daughter due to your verbal claim?'

'Hey, no person's forcing you to do whatever, and I am no longer soliciting for her hand in marriage now. We most effective get married once I have killed the eight-headed serpent.'

'But you're a god!' the aged woman cried, 'Shouldn't you be rescuing people for gratis?'

'Lady, when you have been a goddess, might also need to you rescue humans with out value? Now, are we able to have a deal, or will we now?'

The three of them sat and negotiated for a long term, with the aged couple ultimately agreeing out of complete and utter desperation. Happy with how topics had grew to become out, Susanoo planned out what he might do next. 'How need to I do this?' He mused as the aged couple glared. 'Zap it with lightning? Summon a big flood to drown it? Wait, wait! I need to rain flayed horses on its heads. Now that is probably fun…'

After some time, he finally makes a selection to method the fight with a combination of wit, magic, and uncooked may. Only at that thing could not it befit his reputation due to the fact the can also Shinto God of storms and provoke the hearts of the humans.

The first step of his plan supposed he had to rework Kushinada-Hime, the last daughter, right into a comb and placed her in his hair to preserve her steady. Since he become a typhoon god, his mane of hair emerge as generally perfectly raveled chaos continuously.

Then he suggested that a hedge want to be built that encircled a big venture. It become to have 8 separate gates built into it.

Next, he informed the couple to brew up sufficient sake to fill eight massive tubs and to vicinity the ones tubes throughout the barren location for Orochi to find out and drink. Specifically, one tube for each hand. With the brewing abilities of the couple, and the whole thing else intending as he had deliberate, it wouldn't be prolonged before the serpent is probably drunk.

Susanoo sheltered away, searching forward to Orochi to reach. Suddenly, ominous crammed the vicinity. Dark, eerie clouds revel in across the area, with thunder and lightning following. They have been soon inside the midst of a typhoon. The land changed into rocked by way of massive tremors. The hills spherical them crumbled in advance than their very eyes, and wood had been mowed down, making terrible sounds. Then the monster modified into in advance than them. His breaths grow to be windstorms.

For some time, Orochi stood there and sniffed the air. Lured with the aid of the candy heady scent of the sake, Orochi commenced out to drink all the wine greedily. Each head become taking care of their non-public vat. It wasn't lengthy in advance than he have become under the effect of alcohol and dozing inside the center of the hedge, snoring loudly.

After this, Susanoo crept to the serpent and consequences lopped off each head the use of his large sward. Just be at the stable side, he moreover diced up the frame of the serpent. He felt that the beef might possibly make for a quite umai serpent sashimi during the wedding.

'What is this!' he shouted at the same time as his sword modified into stopped with the useful useful resource of some thing tough in the tail of the Orochi. When he checked his blade, he observed a deep notch in it. Something deep within Orochi have been steely sufficient to dent the brink of this magical sword. Had it been his backbone? Maybe Orochi had eaten some ore? No, that couldn't be it. Who should take delivery of as true with it? After he sliced away the the rest of his flesh, Susanoo located a amazing sword embedded within the tail of Orochi. One take a look at this deadly blade and Susanoo knew the sword had no same existence. With his godly knowledge, Susanoo knew that this sword might be capable of live on all the time in myths and legends.

'Danna,' Kushinada-Hime whispered with fear in Susanoo's hair as he marveled on the blade. 'A sword in a dull snake. Is this an omen that you're going to be an abusive husband? Should I be involved and start looking for caves to cowl in?'

'Nonsense, silly girl,' Susanoo grinned. 'This will make sure that we stay on forever within the hearts of mortals near and an extended way. Think approximately it. Who else might also find out a mythical weapon this way? Everybody else just shoots them from afar.'

And so it grow to be because the God of Storms had predicted. The sword in the snake have turn out to be referred to as Ame-no-Murakumo-no-Tsurugi and have become one of the maximum well-known swords in Japanese records. This became the sword Susanoo may additionally in the long run supply to his sister Amaterasu, who could gift the sword to the first-rate Japanese warrior-emperor Yamato Takeru. Today, this mythical blade is respected as one of the Three Imperial Regalia of Japan. The lifestyles of this blade represents the divine connection a number of the Japanese Royal Family and the Gods of Shinto. As Susanoo foresaw, the story of the first rate discovery keeps to encourage many these days.

After he defeated Orochi, Susanoo married Kushinada and settled into Izumo. Susanoo would possibly compose a poem in honor of his new partner and the land of Izumo. This poem is considered to be the primary Waka in recorded records."

Chapter 7: The Tongue-Cut Sparrow

"Many, some years in the past in Japan, there lived an antique guy and his wife. The senior fellow modified into a hard-going for walks, type-hearted, and appropriate older man, however that changed into the case for his associate. She became a ordinary flow-patch. She need to damage the happiness of her home truely through scolding. She grow to be continuously fussing about some issue from day tonight. The vintage guy had gotten used to her crossness and didn't even word it anymore. He worked most of the times within the fields, and, thinking about the truth that that they'd no kids, for his leisure at the identical time as he again home, he took care of a tame sparrow. He cared about that little chicken actually as an lousy lot as if she had been his little one.

Each night time time, on the same time as he returned domestic after a hard day's artwork inside the out of doors, it turn out to be his quality delight to get to pet his sparrow, to talk together together with her, and to train her a few easy hints, which she end up capable of choose up proper away. He would possibly open up her cage and permit her to fly around the room, and they may play for some time collectively. Once it have come to be supper time, he ought to usually shop some bits from his plate that he may also use to feed his little chook.

There modified into someday whilst the antique guy went out into the wooded place to cut a few wood, and the antique woman stopped at home to easy their clothes. The day earlier than, she had blended up some glowing starch, and now that she have end up searching out it, it have emerge as all long past. The bowl which have been stuffed entire the previous day have become completely empty. While she was looking to discern out who may also moreover need to have stolen or used all of the starch, down flew her husband's puppy sparrow. She bowed her little feathered head, which she were taught through her draw close, the quite bird chirped and said, 'It is I who've taken the starch. I idea it became some food placed out for me in that basin, and I ate it all. If I clearly have made a mistake, I beg you to forgive me! Tweet, tweet, tweet.'

You can see via the sparrow's actions that it have end up a honest bird, and the older lady, if she have been a kindly lady, ought to have been willing to forgive her whilst she requested her pardon so nicely. But that is not what the vintage female did.

The antique girl had in no way cared for the sparrow and had fought together with her husband on numerous sports about keeping what she may want to frequently call a grimy chook approximately the residence. She said that it simplest did more paintings for her. Now she modified into exceptional too satisfied to have some thing to whinge about toward the pup. She scolded or maybe cursed the terrible little hen for the way she had acted, and now not satisfied with just her difficult, unfeeling terms, in a wholesome of rage, she grabbed up the sparrow. The sparrow had remained along facet her wings spread out, and her head bowed in advance than the antique woman as she grow to be scolded to reveal how sorry she have become. Once the old female had the sparrow in hand, she grabbed more than one scissors and reduce off the hen's tongue.

'I meant you took my starch with that tongue! Now you may see what it is like to move with out it!' With those terms, she drove the birds away, not being involved in any respect what might also come of the bird and with out the tiniest bit of pity for its struggling.

The antique girl, as quick as she had raced the sparrow away, blended up some more rice-paste, grumbling the complete time approximately all the hassle, and as quick as she starched all of the clothes, she unfold them out on boards to dry inside the sun as opposed to ironing them.

Once the middle of the night came, the antique guy made his way home. As modified into ordinary for him, at the way decrease again, he seemed ahead to the time at the same time as he ought to get to the gate and spot his pet come chirping to fulfill him, ruffling up her feathers to show her happiness earlier than coming to land on his shoulder. Tonight, even though, the antique guy modified into disenchanted, for he didn't even see the shadow of his sparrow.

He picked up his pace, and unexpectedly pulled off his straw sandals earlier than stepping onto the veranda. Still, he could not see a sparrow. He felt for positive that his spouse, in surely certainly one of her pass tempers, had locked the sparrow up in its cage. He referred to as out to her and said anxiously, 'Where is Suzume San nowadays?'

The antique lady decided to play dumb and pretend to not recognize what had occurred, and spoke back with, 'Your sparrow? I am high-quality I don't apprehend. Now I come to consider it, and I haven't visible her all that afternoon. I shouldn't wonder if the ungrateful fowl had flown away and left you anyhow your petting!'

But the antique man would possibly now not offer his spouse any peace on the situation. Instead, he should ask again and again in which the chicken end up, insisting that she had to apprehend what have turn out to be of his pet. She finally confessed to what she had finished. She recommended him crossly how the sparrow had eaten all the rice- paste that she had made in particular for starching the clothes and the manner the sparrow had advised her the entirety. Then she knowledgeable him how, in superb anger, she had taken scissors and decrease out the chicken's tongue, and the manner she had ultimately driven the bird away and forbade her to head returned to their house ever another time.

She then pulled out the sparrow's tongue and stated, 'Here is the tongue I cut off! Horrid little fowl, why did it devour all of my starch?'

'How ought to you ever be so merciless? Oh, how might also moreover want to you be so merciless?' That have become all that the antique man should muster. He have become too kind-hearted to punish his shrew of a partner however is as a substitute disappointed approximately what had been achieved to his horrific little sparrow.

'What a dreadful misfortune for my horrible Suzume San to lose her tongue!' he muttered to himself. 'She won't be capable of chirp any more, and genuinely the ache of the reducing of it out in that tough way must have made her sick! Is there not some thing to be achieved?'

Once his move companion had fallen asleep for the night time time, the antique guy shed many tears. As he wiped away the tears with the sleeve of his gown, a vibrant concept came to him. He end up going to go out and search for the sparrow at the morrow. Having made this desire, he in the end want to go to sleep.

The following morning he awoke early as speedy as sunlight hours broke. After he grabbed a brief breakfast, he commenced out over the hills and thru the woods. He ought to prevent at each unmarried clump of bamboo to cry out, 'Where, oh in which, does my tongue-lessen sparrow live? Where, oh in which, does my tongue-reduce sparrow stay?'

He didn't prevent to rest for his lunch, and it modified into very overdue into the afternoon at the same time as he determined himself near a large bamboo thicket. Bamboo groves are one of the maximum favored places for sparrows, and quality sufficient, at the edge of the wood, he located his pricey sparrow ready to welcome him. He couldn't recall his eyes and ran at once for her to greet her. She bowed her little head and went through all of the pointers that she have been taught to expose her happiness in getting to see her vintage friend over again. To the antique guy's wonder, she can also need to speak similar to earlier than.

The vintage man apologized to her and for what had happened and asked how she have to communicate so splendidly without it. The sparrow opened up her beak and showed him that she had a new tongue that had grown in location of the antique one. She begged him not to reflect onconsideration on the past anymore, for she have become quite properly. The vintage man fast realized that his sparrow turn out to be a fairy and now not a commonplace chicken. It is probably difficult to exaggerate how glad the individual end up right now. He forgot approximately all of his problems. He even forgot approximately how tired he turned into, for he had eventually placed his cherished misplaced sparrow. Instead of being ill and with out her tongue, due to the fact the vintage man had feared, she end up glad and properly with a current tongue. She had no sign of the ill-remedy she had received from his spouse. Above all else, she become a fairy.

The sparrow asked the vintage man to conform with her and to fly certainly inside the the front of him, and she or he or he led him to a outstanding house within the center of the bamboo grove. The antique guy end up thoroughly greatly surprised at the equal time as he walked into the residence. He determined that it become a adorable vicinity. It were constituted of the whitest of timber. The gentle cream-coloured mats, that have been positioned down in location of the carpets, were the nicest he had ever visible. The cushions that the sparrow delivered to the person to take a seat upon were product of the best silk and crape. Lacquer packing containers and notable vases embellished the tokonoma of every room.

The sparrow took the antique guy to the area of honor, and then, taking her one spot at a humble distance, she thanked the antique guy with many polite bows for all of his kindness that he had given her for such an entire lot of lengthy years. Then, Lady Sparrow known as in her family and introduced them to the vintage guy.

After the introductions had been finished, her daughters sporting dainty crape gowns added in a dinner party of delicious food on antique college trays. They introduced in a lot meals that the vintage guy belief he needed to be dreaming. In the center of their dinner, a number of the sparrow's daughters finished a great dance this is called the Suzume-Odori, or 'the Sparrow's dance,' to entertain the visitor.

Never had the antique guy had lots fun? The hours flew via a whole lot too rapid in this lovely location with all of the fairy sparrows to wait upon him, feed him, and dance for him.

But while the night came, the darkness reminded the vintage guy that he had a totally prolonged manner to stroll and want to think about taking his go away and getting lower back domestic. He thanked all of his kindly the hostess for her amazing amusement and begged her that she ought to forget about approximately approximately all approximately what had passed off to her at the fingers of his move wife. He advised Lady Sparrow this is changed proper right into a incredible consolation and happiness to him to locate that she had such an amazing domestic and to apprehend that she desired for nothing. He described, no longer knowing what had happened to her and the manner she fared induced him anxiety. He now knew that each one changed into properly and that he should go back home with a mild coronary coronary heart. He informed her that if she ever wanted some thing from him, she had only to deliver for him, and he would possibly come right away.

The Lady Sparrow begged the antique guy to stay and rest with them for severa days and experience the alternate of pace, however the antique guy defined that he needed to go back to his antique partner, who would possibly probably be very disenchanted for the truth that he hadn't again domestic at his normal time. He moreover desires to flow lower lower back to his wore, and as such, regardless of how an lousy lot he desired he may additionally want to acquire this, he couldn't accept the invitation to stay. Now that he knew wherein his loved Lady Sparrow lived, he could come to go to her on every occasion he had time.

Once Lady Sparrow noticed that she can be not in a role to influence the vintage man to stay, she gave an order to some of the servants, and that they brought in containers. One field turn out to be big, and one modified into small. These were set in advance than the vintage man, and the Lady Sparrow requested him to pick out out whichever one of the boxes he favored for a present. The antique guy couldn't turn this idea and picked out the smaller of the 2 bins.

He defined his choice through saying, 'I am now too vintage and feeble to preserve the huge and heavy field. As you are so kind as to say that I can also moreover take whichever I like, I will select the small one, for you to be simpler for me to hold.'

All of the sparrows helped him location the container on his over again, and they accompanied him to the gate to look him off, bidding him farewell with many bows. They requested him to move back again each time he had the time. Thus the antique man left his pup sparrow pretty luckily. The sparrow did no longer show the least bit of sick-will for all of the unkindness that she had persevered at the fingers of his vintage spouse. Indeed, the great component she felt modified into sorrow for the vintage guy who needed to deal with it all of the time.

Once the antique man were given again to his domestic, he decided his spouse crosser than general, for it became very past due in the night time time, and he or she have been ready up for him to get home.

'Where have you ever ever ever been all this time?' she asked with anger in her voice. 'Why do you come so past due?'

The vintage guy attempted to calm his associate down through showing her the sector of offers that he had decrease once more with, after which told her the whole thing had took place to him, and the way wonderful it had been to be entertained at the sparrow's residence.

'Now let us see what is in the container,' the antique man stated, no longer giving her the risk to grouse all all over again. 'You ought to assist me open it.' They every sat down in the front of the sector and opened it.

To their amazement, the field modified into filled to brim with silver and gold cash and plenty of different treasured gadgets. The mats of the little cottage glittered as they eliminated all the gadgets, one after the other, and placed them down and handled them again and again. The vintage man emerge as conquer with satisfaction on the sight of the whole lot that turn out to be now his. The sparrow's present end up beyond his wildest dream. It became going to allow him to give up his paintings and live in ease and luxury for the relaxation of his existence.

He stated, 'Thanks to my accurate little sparrow! Thanks to my suitable little sparrow!' He repeated this word over and over another time.

But 'Twas the vintage woman's evil nature, after the number one few moments of delight and marvel had worn off, and she or he could not suppress her greed. She started accountable the vintage guy for not having delivered once more the large discipline of offers. He had innocently advised her how he had refused the bigger of the 2 boxes, who choose the smaller one because it might be lighter and less complicated to keep.

'You silly antique man,' stated the antique female, 'Why did you not deliver the huge discipline? Just think about what we've had been given misplaced. We may additionally additionally have had two times as plenty silver and gold as this. You are really an vintage fool!' She screamed and huffed to mattress in anger.

The old guy now needed that he had by no means cited some aspect approximately the larger container, however it turn out to be too overdue now. The greedy vintage female, now not glad with their suitable well fortune that had suddenly befallen them, and which she did no longer deserve, made up her mind to get extra.

Very early the subsequent morning, she awoke and made the vintage guy tell her the manner to get to the sparrow's domestic. Once he determined out what she grow to be planning on doing, he tried to hold her from going, but it have grow to be of no need. She grow to be no longer going to concentrate to a word he stated. It become ordinary how the vintage female didn't feel the least bit ashamed of going to visit the sparrow after how cruelly she had treated her. But all of that greed she had for the huge area made her neglect about the whole thing else. It did even dawn on her that the sparrows may be irritated together together with her, which they were, and can punish her for what she had finished.

Ever because of the truth the second the Lady Sparrow had decrease lower back to her home in the sad kingdom that her own family had decided her, bleeding and weeping from the mouth, her entire circle of relatives had completed little extra than talk approximately how evil the vintage lady became. 'How need to she?' they asked every different, 'inflict this kind of heavy punishment for any such trifling offense as that of consuming a few rice-paste via mistake? ' The loved the vintage guy very hundreds, who they knew became kind and acceptable and affected man or woman under all of the problems he had. But they despised the vintage girl, and they determined that in the occasion that they ever had the threat, they may punish her as she deserved. They did not have prolonged to wait.

After she walked for plenty hours, the antique female got here upon the bamboo grove which she had demanded her husband cautiously describe. She stood earlier than it and shouted, 'Where is the tongue-cut sparrow's residence? Where is the tongue-reduce sparrow's house?'

At very last, she found the eaves of the house poking out from between the bamboo foliage. She raced to the door and knocked loudly. Once, the servants informed the Lady Sparrow that her vintage mistress turned into on the door, asking or her. She modified into pretty surprised at this surprising visit. After the whole lot that had came about, she did now not surprise a chunk on the boldness of the vintage female in coming to her residence. The Lady Sparrow, but, have grow to be polite, and so she ventured out to greet the vintage woman, remembering that she became as soon as her mistress.

The vintage lady did now not intend to waste any time, and she or he got right now to the thing without any shame in any respect. She stated, 'You need not trouble to entertain me as you in all likelihood did, my vintage man. I truely have come myself to get the container which he so stupidly left in the back of. I shall quick take my leave if you supply me the big concern. This is all I want!'

The Lady Sparrow consented and called to her servants to supply out the large problem. The vintage girl eagerly grabbed the box and hoisted onto her another time. Without even thanking the Lady Sparrow, she began to hurry domestic.

The field modified into so hefty that she could not walk rapid, a whole lot tons much less run, as she favored to do. She became aggravating to get domestic and see what become indoors of the box, but she positioned that she had to sit down and rest now and again.

As she staggered underneath her heavy load, her preference to open up the box have become too splendid to face as much as. She couldn't wait until she have been given domestic due to the reality she assumed that it become a field entire of silver and gold, treasured jewels just like the small one had been.

At closing, all of her greed and selfishness made her placed the container down and open it carefully. She expected to brag her eyes upon a mine of wealth. What she observed, but, so terrified her that she nearly lost all of her senses. As quickly as she removed the lid, severa terrifying and frightful searching demons bounced out of the box and surrounded her, looking as although they purported to kill her. Never in her worst dreams had she ever visible such terrible looking creatures. A demon that had one large eye inside the center of its brow came beforehand and glared on the antique lady. Monsters that had gaping mouths appeared like they were going to consume her. A huge snake coiled and hissed round her, and a extremely good frog hopped and croaked toward her.

The older girl had in no way felt so concerned in her lifestyles and ran a long manner from that spot as speedy as her legs might also moreover want to probable carry her, satisfied to interrupt out alive. Once she reaches the house, she fell to the ground and suggested her husband via tears about the whole thing that had came about to her, and the manner she had almost been killed through the demons and monsters that have been inside the area.

Then she commenced responsible the sparrow, but the antique guy fast stopped her. He said, 'Don't blame the sparrow. It is your wickedness, which has at final met with its praise. I terrific desire this could be a lesson for you inside the future!'

The vintage girl did now not replay, and from that day ahead, she repented of her pass, unkind behavior. She end up a very good vintage lady in order that her husband hardly ever recognized her because the identical individual, and they spend the have a study in their lives fortuitously, free from care or need, spending the treasures cautiously that the antique man had gotten from his doggy, the tongue-lessen sparrow."

Chapter 8: The Peach Boy – Momotaro

"A long time in the beyond, there lived an antique girl and an antique man. They have been peasants and labored difficult to earn their rice every day. The vintage man might also want to move and cut grass for the farmers throughout the town. While he became doing this, his spouse did the house obligations and worked in their little rice subject.

One day, the person went into the hills to reduce grass, and his wife took a few garments all the manner all the way down to the river to wash them.

It come to be nearly summer time, and america modified into lovely. It have become fresh for them to appearance all the greenness as they went to work. The grass beside the river regarded like green velvet, and the pussy willows on the point of the water stood shaking their easy tassels.

The breeze blew and ruffled the water's floor. This grew to become the water into small waves. The breeze passed alongside and touched the cheeks of the vintage couple who felt very happy this specific morning. The antique couple didn't apprehend why they have been so thrilled, they just knew they had been.

The lady in the end determined a gap on the river monetary institution and located her basket on the floor. She then commenced running on washing the garments. She took every object out of the basket one at a time and washed them inside the river. She rubbed them at the stones to get them easy. The water end up crystal easy, and she should see the small fish swimming all spherical. She also can see each pebble on the lowest.

While she end up washing their garments, a huge peach came bumping down the motion. She appeared up from washing the garments and observed the peach. She changed into 60 years vintage, and she hadn't ever seen a peach this length in all of her existence.

She idea to herself, 'How delicious that peach have to be! I want to get it and take it home to my husband.'

She reached her arm out and tried to lure it, however it changed into out of her obtain. She regarded spherical for a stick, but there wasn't one which she need to see. If she went seeking out a stick, she could lose the peach.

She stopped for a 2d to consider what she have to do, and then she remembered an antique enchantment. So, she started to clap her fingers to preserve time with the rolling peach taking place the circulate. While she clapped, she sang this track:

'Distant water is bitter, and the close to water is satisfactory; skip thru the far off water and are to be had into the candy.'

It have grow to be uncommon to mention that as brief as she started out repeating this song, the peach started out out getting nearer and closer to the river financial organization in which she became fame. It in the end stopped proper inside the front of her in order that she might also need to pick it up together along with her arms. She end up so excited. She couldn't cease the showering due to the fact she changed into too excited and glad. She placed all the clothes another time within the basket and slung the basket onto her decrease again. She carried the peach in her fingers and moved quickly home.

It regarded like a totally long term until her husband again domestic. He modified into finally yet again home genuinely because the solar started out out to set. He had a big package deal of grass on his back. It emerge as so large that he have emerge as almost hidden with the useful resource of the usage of it. She nearly couldn't see him. He seemed very tired and have become the usage of the scythe as a taking walks stick. He became leaning on it as he walked alongside.

When the vintage female observed him, she known as out to him.

'Oh, Fii San! I had been ready as a way to come home for one of these long time in recent times!'

'What is the hassle? Why are you so impatient?' he requested, wondering at her eagerness that have emerge as very unusual. 'Has something happened even as I modified into away?'

'Oh, no!' she answered. 'Nothing has came about. I just positioned a nice present for you!'

'That is right.' stated the antique man. He then washed his feet in a basin of water and stepping onto the veranda.

The woman bumped into the little room and taken out the peach from the cupboard. It felt heavier than it did in advance. He held it as plenty as him and said:

'Just study this! Did you ever see a peach this huge for your life?'

When he looked at the peach, he became astonished and said:

'This is certainly the most essential peach I actually have ever seen! Wherever did you buy it?'

'I did no longer buy it.' she spoke back. 'I observed it inside the river in which I changed into washing the garments.'

She proceeded to inform him the story of the way she changed into capable of get the peach.

'I am thrilled which you have placed it. Let us eat it now, for I am hungry.' stated the antique man.

He took out a kitchen knife and placed the peach on a cutting board. She was pretty plenty to reduce into it even as all of sudden the peach split in , and a easy voice said:

'Wait a bit, antique man!' To their marvel, a stunning toddler stepped out of the peach.

The antique woman and her husband were astonished at what that they had visible that they fell down. The infant spoke one more time:

'Don't be afraid. I am no demon or fairy. I will let you know the truth. Heaven has had compassion on you. Every day and each night time time, you have got lamented which you had no child. Your cry has been heard, and I am despatched to be the son of your vintage age!'

Upon taking note of this, the antique woman and her husband had been overjoyed. They had cried day and night time time time with sorrow at no longer having a infant to assist them in their antique age. Now their prayers had been replied; they had been so entire of delight that they didn't apprehend what to do with their feet or their arms. The antique man picked the child up in his hands and then surpassed him to the antique female. They gave him the selection of Momotaro or Son of a Peach considering the truth that he got here out of a peach.

Years exceeded quick, and the kid grew sturdy. He was 15 years vintage, and he modified into taller and extra strong than some other boy his age. He have become handsome and very brave. He have turn out to be clever for his age, too. The couple's pleasure became so first-rate once they looked at him. He have end up what they believed a hero need to appear to be.

Momotaro comes to his father within the destiny and solemnly stated:

'Father, with the useful resource of the usage of a weird threat, we've grow to be father and son. Your goodness to me has been higher than the mountain grasses which it have come to be your each day art work to reduce, and deeper than the river wherein my mother washes the clothes. I do no longer understand a way to thanks enough.'

'Why,' the vintage guy said, 'it's miles a rely of course that a father need to hold up his a few. When you're antique, it will probable be your flip to take care of us, so anyhow, there may be no profits or loss among us as everybody might be identical. Indeed, I am as an alternative surprised that you have to thank me in this manner!' the antique guy started searching troubled.

'I wish you'll be patient with me,' stated Momotaro, 'but earlier than I begin to pay again your goodness to me, I truly have a request to make which I need you may provide me above the entirety else.'

'I will permit you to perform a little factor you need, for you are pretty one in each of a kind from all the one of a kind boys!'

'Then permit me go away at once!'

'What do you are saying? Do you need to transport away your vintage mother and father and move faraway from your antique domestic?'

'I will honestly come once more yet again in case you allow me skip now!'

'Where are you going?'

'You have to count on it bizarre that I want to go away,' Momotaro stated, 'due to the reality I simply have no longer but counseled you my purpose. Far far from here to the northeast of Japan, there's an island within the sea. This island is the stronghold of a band of devils. I sincerely have regularly heard how they invade this land, kill and rob the people, and produce off all they may find out. They are not incredible evil, however they will be disloyal to our Emperor and disobey his criminal pointers. They are also cannibals, for they kill and consume some of the horrible folks that are so unlucky as to fall into their arms. These devils are very evil beings. I must circulate and conquer them and bring decrease lower back all of the plunder of which they have got robbed this land. It is because of this that I need to move away for a brief time!'

Chapter 9: History Of Japan

Usually, the subdivision of Japanese history takes area in AGE = Time durations (e.g., prehistoric); PERIODS OR PERIODS, which may be lesser durations than the previous ones but can skip from many years to centuries. Historians normally gave the name to the Periods based totally on the seat of government.

It is commonplace in Japan to signify the years no longer via a single uninterrupted numerical succession however a chain of eras (lasting a few years) and a revolutionary great type of years interior each length (nengô). This device remains applied in Japan (especially in information books and proper documents), but it is increasingly more supported thru the Western gadget for all sensible uses.

It want to be mentioned that the denomination of the epochs and ancient intervals and their temporal limits aren't specific. In precise, the subdivision used inside the statistics of artwork isn't always similar to that adopted for political information. Therefore, we need to now not be amazed if we come across unique periodization from the most effective.

JOMON PERIOD (about 10,000-3 hundred BC)

The Jomon duration advanced round 10,000 BC as an awful lot as 3 hundred BC located in its first population in particular nomads, men continuously shifting from the coasts to inland areas and dedicated (giving sufficient development) to agriculture, searching, and fishing as this very last became the precept electricity deliver. They additionally created embellished clay pots, frequently with a way that worried the use of ropes pressed at the even though-damp clay. Some of the oldest specimens are determined in Japan.

YAYOI PERIOD (3 hundred BC-250AD)

In chronological order comes the Yayoi period, which is going from 3 hundred BC to 250 AD. And whose call derives from the

Tokyo district in which archaeological remains of the era were placed for the primary time (inside the musical problem, for example, flutes, lyres, and stringed devices). We have severa property approximately the start of this period; some characteristic it to the the front of rice cultivation in paddy fields, others to new types of pottery. Mainly it superior in the southern area of Kyushu and northern Honshu. Recent discoveries, but, advise that the Yayoi length started out spherical 900 BC. Furthermore, immigrants from the East Asian continent delivered the manufacturing of objects in bronze and iron.

KOFUN OR YAMATO PERIOD (about 3 hundred-552 AD)

From 250/3 hundred AD and as much as the middle of 552, it is known as the Kofun period (period of the Tumuli, taking its name from the feature mound tombs on Earth and Stone that had special sizes regular with the social fame of the deceased and contained the gadgets maximum high-priced to them inner.

: ceramics, armor, and guns, on the equal time as externally, you may see internally empty clay statuettes referred to as "haniwa" and to which one-of-a-type roles have been attributed: from sentinels of the grave to substitutes for the servants who've been buried alive with the noble. The authorities took extra power, collectively with turning into imperial lineage and being in the apparent of Yamato took its name (Sun Yamato). Through this dynasty, there was the unification of Japan.

ASUKA PERIOD (550-710)

This period shows the primary Buddhist duration inside the records of this america of the us which have come to be delivered from Korea; conventionally enclosed among 550 and seven hundred while there has been the switch of the capital to Nara from which it took its call, for this reason identifying a profound have an impact on of precis idealism on the entire way of life of Japan. According to a few, the period ended while Emperor

Tenji came to the throne round 667. Before the forestall of the century, the capital have become relocated numerous times. In 701, the exquisite Taiho Ritsuryo codes were finished, which would have done a feature of outstanding importance. Inside the subsequent Nara length.

NARA PERIOD (710-794)

In this unique period (which took its call from the primary regular capital inside the northwestern place of the Yamato simple and moreover called Heijiokyo, built via Emperor Gemmei). Japan have come to be an crucial region at the Silk Road and had a first rate cultural development because of the Tang dynasties and the assimilation of Chinese subculture. There were severa introductions: ideographic writing, the writing of internal chronicles inside the the us, and a code of laws known as "Tahio," land reform. The u . S . Changed into politically divided into provinces, districts, and villages. The immoderate creative degree finished in the ones years thru the use of completing the temple of the brilliant Buddha of Nara and the big building that houses this adorable sculpture, the Todaiji temple, is the maximum giant wooden advent in the worldwide.

HEIAN PERIOD (795-1185)

The duration affirmed its very personal way of life with models and traditions everyday of the usa; additionally reigned peace, prosperity, and vital families had been born (inclusive of that of the Fujiwara, who exercised influentially from 866 to 882). While a massive improvement in artwork, poetry, and literature immortalized by means of the court docket woman, Murasaki Shikibu inside the Genji Monogatari (The Tale of Genji) showed one of the oldest extant reminiscences. The first famous samurai warriors were moreover born. Another important thing turned into the capital's waft to Kyoto (ancient name Heian). In religion, however, there has been such propagation of Buddhism that it have emerge as protected with country wide existence. A new aristocracy specifically interested in agriculture sought to suitable land formerly legally given to many small farmers. All this due to the truth he loved various tax benefits and became temperamentally warlike. Two have come to be the most influential families: the Minamoto and the Taira. The latter have come to be so effective that they killed the Fujiwara, and in order that they needed to struggle with the Minamoto, who acquired the fantastic war of Dan-Noura, setting up a golden age for cavalry.

KAMAKURA PERIOD (1185-1333)

In this era, the electricity surpassed to the military elegance became just like the feudal device of the Middle Ages in Europe. There had been many big sports: the importation of Zen Buddhism, the transformation in clothing that went from wealthy to light clothing, the propagation of the "Song" architectural fashion, and the resumption of contributors of the own family with China. In 1192 the

"Shogun" have become born with the generalissimo Minamoto, which lasted till 1867. He proclaimed Kamakura the capital and created an absolute dictatorship. Thus ended the imperial regime, and the shogunate come to be covered, however it fragmented exactly in this era. The successors or the effective Hojo prolonged circle of relatives, have been able to address non-stop Mongol invasions round 1274 and 1281, repelling them also helped via a hurricane that the Japanese interpreted as a Kamikaze or moreover called "Divine Wind," but developing in the ruling class, a loss of guide from the warriors.

MUROMACHI PERIOD (1333-1576)

It started out with the Emperor Go-Daigo, who reigned till, following a rise up led with the aid of the shogun warrior Ashikaga he modified into pressured to take safe haven at the heights. It have become because of the shortage of determination with which he reigned until round 1573 and handiest due to the truth, within the period in-between, no characters worth of prevarication emerged that, collectively with the growing boom of Buddhist monasteries with their armies, the Ashikaga kingdom with its descendants and Japan slid into civil war and chaos. In this era, it have turn out to be essential for the development of a category of wholesale traders, usurers and coins changers, transporters, the resumption of commercial enterprise members of the circle of relatives with the continent previously interrupted, and the touchdown of customers and missionaries, Spanish and Portuguese inside the course of 1542 who they brought Christianity which without delay unfold.

MOMOYAMA PERIOD (1576-1600)

Thanks to three warriors of modest origins, Japan reached reunification and entered a new historic segment, bringing it with the help of the army in the direction of a unitary one. This chapter of records takes its call from the fort of the equal call. However, after a massive and taken into attention threatening spread, ruthless repression commenced out for Christianity.

TOKUGAWA PERIOD: (1600-1867)

It come to be within the early sixteenth century. With the Portuguese, Christianity arrived in Japan, growing in the reigning Hideyoshi Toyotomi this type of problem for the developing popularity that they drove out the missionaries and suppressed 26 Christians as a caution. These emotions moreover on the a part of the government did not lessen over the years. In this era (1600-1867), Tokugawa Ieyasu defeated the younger inheritor Hideyoshi, organising his headquarters in Edo (current Tokyo) and from which he also took his call (from 1603 to 1867) and, greater exactly, in 1614 additionally to restrict and disarm the financial integration of the Dutch in Japan. Christianity have emerge as outlawed, persecuting and killing (hundreds have been the patients) individuals who stored their religion, other than small minorities on the extra Japanese territory, resisted in Nagasaki; in the intervening time, the emperor persisted to exercising fine formal authority in Kyoto. This Tokugawa own family introduced Japan right right into a duration of isolation: they were forbidden to transport foreign places and change with other worldwide places, even as foreigners were subjected to strict surveillance. The significance of in truth submitting to the tips of obedience and constancy, an component even though present inside the Japanese mentality, changed into affirmed. Decisive political and social modifications within the nineteenth century were due to wealthy shoppers who desired to take some distance more crucial positions than those due. At the identical time, severa samurai started out out to exchange and do specific jobs for the low salaries they had.

There have been improvements within the reforms made with the beneficial resource of the shogun Togukawa Nariaki even though their effects had been blocked due to office work. A intense calamity which encompass famine struck the usa for about ten years, developing a scenario near a rebellion through way of the human beings. Meanwhile, the emperor's devoted formed a modern-day that blamed the failure on Western pressure to open diplomatic and business participants of the circle of relatives.

Later calamities collectively with famine brought on popular uprisings to be feared till Tokugawa Nariaki of the shogun dynasty started out out a chain of reforms, however one-of-a-type currents accused him of lack of capability.

MEIJI PERIOD (1868–1912)

Subsequently, from 1868 to 1912, the Meiji Emperor reigned, invested with political electricity after centuries (or period of the enlightened kingdom, i.E., the 45 years of the reign of the Meiji Emperor) and, as a result renewing them, finished the preceding reforms with political and social modifications. And western economics in the university, u . S . A ., and criminal sectors through growing a Japanese charter. Christianity emerge as additionally banned subsequently of this reign and till the end of World War II. After a brief technique of industrialization in 1889, the cutting-edge-day constitution turned into born, on the identical time as in 1904, there was the interruption of diplomatic members of the circle of relatives with Russia and the ensuing battle that marked for the primary time the Asian victory over a European u.S. And reinforced the opinion on the Japanese. It specially sided with the allies in World War I to boom its financial device through change.

TAISHO PERIOD (1912-1926)

In 1912, Emperor Taisho ascended the throne, moreover starting a period that took his name however have become no longer so authoritarian as to avoid opposite currents. In 1923, however, the towns of Tokyo and Yokohama and their environment had been hit thru a effective earthquake. The lack of lifestyles of the emperor ended this period.

SHOWA PERIOD (1926-1945)

When Emperor Hirohito ascended the throne, the us of a suffered an financial disaster that gave greater strength to the military. After the second one conflict in competition to China, this allied itself and signed a percentage with Italy and Germany. Then there has been the no matter the truth that famous surprise assault on Pearl Harbor in 'forty one in competition to the USA that a 12 months later became the tide with the naval struggle of Midway, forcing them to retreat. TARDA SHOWA modified into described from 1945 to 1989, and a reform sanctioned the right of ladies. Then in August 1945, at the same time as Japan modified into withdrawn, there had been the declaration of battle with the useful aid of the Soviet Union and the dropping of atomic bombs on Hiroshima and Nagasaki, which ended the struggle and made the emperor sign an unconditional surrender.

Then discovered a huge healing period in all sectors: company and the financial device. However, the military profession ended most effective in 1952, while he entered the UN in 1956.

HEISEI PERIOD (1989)

The current era started out out while the daddy died, and Emperor Akihito ascended to the throne in January 1989. Tokyo subway introduced on the demise of 12 humans and intoxicated approximately 6000. In 'ninety one, Japan financially supported the Gulf War and sent professionals to defuse mines; squaddies have been despatched to assist rebuild Iraq.

Japanese statistics has been marked thru manner of alternating intervals of isolation and radical outside influences. Its way of existence in recent times is a aggregate of outdoor forces and inner traits.

RELIGIONS THAT HAVE INFLECTED JAPANESE SOCIETY

On the only hand, the Japanese people live their religiosity nearly privately. On the opposite hand, they're capable of share and make precise spiritual cults live together, causing a few confusion for statistical functions.

The maximum giant non secular beliefs in Japan are Shinto and Buddhism, with the alternative non secular office work popularity underneath approximately 10% of the population.

Shinto

Shintoism manner "Way of the Gods." It is a polytheistic and animist faith that does not contemplate sacred texts but is exceeded down orally through Shinto "monks" referred to as kannushi or shinshoku.

Kannushi can be each males and females; they may be capable of marry and feature kids and are commonly answerable for a shrine and kami worship, which we are able to move into in a touch while.

Shinto does not keep in mind the bodily international (kenkai) and the invisible supernatural global (yukai) as divided universes however as coexisting and interacting with each distinct and a part of a unmarried introduction.

State Shinto

During the Meiji period, Shinto have come to be the usa faith, have grow to be separated from Buddhism, and a campaign have emerge as performed to sell country wide identification with the emperor. He became considered a descendant of the goddess Amaterasu.

After World War II, the emperor publicly renounced his reputation as a terrestrial deity and left the divine lineage of the imperial circle of relatives.

What is the Kami?

The Kami (gods or spirits) are the basis of Shinto worship and adoration.

Sometimes there may be a sort of confusion within the expression kami in evaluation to the western gods, and this mistake is because of the phrase's translation.

In clean: by using manner of Kami, the Shinto faith manner all of the ones elements well worth of reverence, whether or not or not they may be gods (even no longer of Japanese starting), spirits of the useless, factors and forces of nature, ancestors, or gadgets of specific significance encompass the charge of the Kami.

Kami are close to human beings as they may be able to have an effect on sports and answer prayers, benevolent or evil, and aren't pleasant entities.

There are over 8 million Kami in Japan, however the huge range may be a long manner more considering that some thing with the functions and virtues to be a kami is appeared.

However, there are a few universally recognized and relevant amongst which:

Amaterasu

Goddess of the Sun.

Izanagi and Izanami

The first man and the number one female gods of introduction.

Fujin

God of the wind.

Hachiman

He is the god of archery and battle.

Tenjin

It is the training-related Kami that one turns to for success in training.

Inari

The deity of agriculture, fertility, and plants.

The Shinto shrines referred to as Jinja (vicinity of the gods) are wherein the Kami are stored. There is mostly a sacred constructing (honden) that homes the Kami and represents the coronary coronary heart of the sanctuary.

These can be of numerous sizes: large, exceedingly small, or maybe transportable and also may be prepared in a network of shrines.

Another detail of brilliant importance inside the sanctuary form is the Torii which represents the entrance portal delimiting the sacred vicinity from the non-sacred one.

After passing the Torii and in advance than moving into the coronary coronary heart of the temple, there are a few purification rituals to be carried out.

Usually, the torii is pink and built with wooden and has an unmistakable form.

Buddhism

Buddhism is a polytheistic faith of Indian beginning based totally totally on the Buddha's teachings and philosophies that purpose to triumph over struggling via a path of liberation and transcendence.

Buddhism got here to Japan thanks to Buddhist clergymen from China and Korea throughout the 6th century AD.

His doctrine modified into well perfect to intertwine with the opportunity religion already gift inside the territory, Shintoism.

Furthermore, being accompanied through the use of a few massive clans and ultimately obtaining the authorities's resource, this creed started to spread with some effectiveness till it have end up included into the territory to discover Shinto and Buddhist cults thing with the beneficial resource of aspect.

The Buddhist schools

There are a couple of Buddhist schools or sects scattered inside the course of Japan, and every of these may be divided into other faculties.

For instance, the numerous many, there are the Tendai school, the Joudo, the Nichiren, the Zen school, the Joudo Shinshu, and the Shingon.

The Zen School and the Nichiren School have spread particularly within the West.

Buddhist temples

The first Buddhist temples have been stimulated with the aid of way of Chinese and Korean shape after which, through the years, reached a greater national identification.

The systems are nearly generally fabricated from wood, with the roof being the primary element.

The interiors are large and can be changed the use of movable partitions.

Some characteristic a pagoda.

You bypass through the Mon (column doorways) to enter the temple, and sacred gadgets are saved in the temple.

Among the famous temples in Japan are those of Todaiji (placed especially in Nara), Sensoji (in Asakusa), Yakushi Ji (in Nara, part of the Buddhist sect Hosso, the oldest in Japan), and Daigo Ji in Kyoto.

Shinbutsu shūgō

Shinbutsu Shugo (Kami and Buddha) is the syncretism among Shinto and Buddhism.

Buddhism arrived in Japan after Shintoism, and as quickly because it modified into delivered in China, a manner changed into sought to make the 2 religions coexist.

Over time they've become associated with such an quantity that that they'd fusion factors; but, following the Meiji Restoration, the 2 cults have been divided, but nonetheless nowadays, in some respects, they'll be complementary.

Religious minorities in Japan

In addition to the 2 outstanding religions said previously, there are drastically fewer, nearly negligible, other cults, in Japan, which includes Christianity, Judaism, Hinduism, and Islam.

Chapter 10: The Principles Of Skiing

Shinto Japanese faith with very historical origins and is associated with the practice of ancestor worship.

Shinto origins

Being enthusiasts of Shintoism does no longer exclude the opportunity of being believers in one of a kind religions. In precise, from the 6th century BC, Shintoism joined and guarded with Buddhism.

Shinto deities

At the idea of the beliefs of the Shinto religion, there may be the Kami (i.E., gods or spirits), whose range is infinitely big. Two deities, Izanagi and sister Izanami, are the begin of Japan. They generated the islands and extraordinary deities. Among the ones, the number one ones are:

Amaterasu,

Susanoo, god of the typhoon;

Tsukiyomi, god of the night;

Kagutsuchi, god of fireside;

Inari, goddess of rice.

Jizo

Jizo is the tremendous determine of children and delivery. It is said that kids who die earlier than their parents cannot pass the mythical Sanzu River into the afterlife because of the truth they have not accumulated enough proper deeds. They are doomed to stack small rocks at the river financial institution all of the time. Jizo allows the kids pass the river via hiding them in his robe. Jizo statues are normally small. They appear in big numbers in temples across Japan. Jizo is also provided with bibs and hats to keep them heat. In a few temples, parents leave toys or stack stones in the the front of Jizo, hoping that their kids might be stable inside the afterlife.

Raijin and Fujin

Raijin is the Kami of large lightning, thunder, and hurricane, typically depicted with hammers and surrounded thru drums. Fujin is the wind kami who's proven with a windbag. Raijin and Fujin frequently appear collectively. They have feared deities due to the harm that typhoons and storms have caused in Japan over the extremely good centuries. Parents historically cautioned their kids to hide their navels in some unspecified time in the future of thunderstorms so Raijin would not consume their bellies. As fearsome deities, each Raijin and Fujin regularly appear alongside the doorways of shrines for safety.

Agyo and Ungyo

Agyo and Ungyo are fearsome guardians of the Buddha who're often determined at the doorway to Japanese temples.

Shinto the crucial beliefs

In every herbal fact, the presence of the divine is perceived, and guy's nature is taken into consideration essentially suitable. Evil is associated with evil spirits, in opposition to whom it's far essential to perform exorcisms and purifying rites. Forms of animism and fetishism are practiced (i.E., the veneration of devices isn't an result in itself but related to correct spirits or demons which are concept to live there), and the veneration of gadgets as material representations of divinity.

Shinto worship and sacred places

The kami worship takes vicinity thru ritual prayers and the supplying of rice and sake. The worship takes place partly in the house on small domestic altars and in part in shrines constructed of wood and normally composed of school rooms related to a prayer room. The honest Shintoist in the the front of this prays after attracting Kami's interest by way of the usage of clapping his palms or ringing a bell. In the principle room, enclosed in a field, there is the shintai, the divine body, that could be a symbol that represents the god (mirror, weapons, and lots of others.).

The number one feature of the Shito chapel is the torii, a yoke portal commonly fabricated from timber and fashioned with the resource of the use of spherical jambs, with two architraves, the very quality of which protrudes beyond the 2 supporting jambs. Torii is on occasion decided at the lakeshore and indicates that the area is sacred.

Shinto: origins and traits

Many sacred places are committed to the Shinto deities, domestic to shrines and a pilgrimage locations. Pilgrims placed on white gowns and rush hats.

Ritual dances are also viral.

Shinto holidays

The holidays are with the resource of and huge related to the harvest and the cycle of nature (the harvest competition, the tasting of new rice). The maximum crucial birthday party is sincerely that of the New Year. On that day, tens of hundreds and heaps of people flock to shrines to wish to the Kami and ask for his or her advantages for the New Year.

Another essential opposition is the cherry blossom festival in early spring.

Shinto sacred texts

The vital ones are mythological texts: Kojki, "Chronicles of historical activities," and Nihongi, "Annals of Japan." Drafted in the 8th century, they deal with the data of Japan from its origins to the 7th century.

Shinto sacred human beings

Worship practices are finished thru way of clergymen (even women can be), who have nearly normally inherited their administrative center from their ancestors. They put on a black cap, a white get dressed, and a cane at some point of the ceremonies.

BUDDHISM IN JAPAN

Buddhism got here to Japan approximately one thousand years after the Buddha via Korea. From the 7th century AD, waves of Buddhism, specifically of the significantly painted Mahavana zenrieta, reached Japan from China. They had been essentially added via Japanese clergymen who had stayed in Chinese monasteries. The maximum popular paperwork that got here this manner are Tendai, Shingon, i.E., a tantric variety, the Pure Land faculties, and the three number one sects of Zen, the Japanese model of Chinese Chan Buddhism: Rinzai, Soto, and Obaku. In the 13th century, the monk Nichiren initiated an completely Japanese shape primarily based on an interpretation of the Lotus Sutra, the precept text of the Tendai.

NEW SCHOOLS OF BUDDHISM

In the final century, new styles of Buddhism have arisen; Buddhism in current Japan, specifically Soki Gakkai, a mundane movement with origins in Nichiren Buddhism. Like many new Japanese non secular actions, Soka Gakkai is excessive-profile) and insists on character and social reform. About 3-quarters of the Japanese population are Buddhists, even though many worships the divine spirit (Kami) of Shinto at domestic.

THE IMPORTANCE OF YOU

Tradition says that the Japanese monk Eisai (1141-1215) 1168 delivered seeds of the tea bush from China and planted them around his temple. Since then, the "manner of tea" (Chado) has been associated with the Rinzai college of Eisai Zen and is an element of Chinese tradition cultivated and converted with the useful resource of Rinzai. In China, tea had already been used to harmonize the body's numerous organs. Although no longer strictly religious, Chado is in element connected with the spirit of Zen: it's miles said that "Zen and tea flavor the identical." Eisai delivered the Rinzai model of Zen to Japan, which seeks a spontaneous form of satori. This Japanese expression way the attainment of enlightenment, completed via a meditative attention on everything.

ZEN BUDDHISM

While not as popular due to the fact the pure Earth or Nichiren-derived colleges, Zen might be the outstanding-recognized shape of Japanese Buddhism in the West. In Japan, it had extensive development and a branch into seven along its eight hundred years of information. Today's essential Zen colleges are Rinzai and Soto; every originated in China. Rinzai is from time to time referred to as the "college of people who shout and beat." This designation derives from the way its founder, Lin-chi, accomplished enlightenment, and masses of recollections circulate about the exuberant demeanor of his masters, who regularly behaved in techniques now not generally allowed. Rinzai's primary meditation exercise specializes within the Koan, an enigmatic saying or query. On the opposite hand, the Soto college emphasizes zazen, "sitting in meditation." According to Dogen (1200-1253), the maximum vital decide in the university's information, zazen must be understood not as a street to enlightenment but as an expression of the kingdom of way of life.

JAPANESE MYTHOLOGY

The founding myths of Shinto are documented in two historical classics. The first is the Kojiki, "antique written subjects," no longer wrongly known as the Japanese Bible. The recollections it contains, passed down orally for loads of years, had been put in writing round seven-hundred AD. The reminiscences of a wonderful Hieda no Are, likely a sacred dancer of the kagura (dramatic representations of the mythological project), were entrusted to us. The noble Ō-no Yasumaro then provided the textual content to Empress Genmyo (708-714). Yasumaro for my part wrote the arrival. The Kojiki gives with the reign of the gods and the introduction of Japan, explains the divine genealogies, after which narrates the legends of the Izumo cycle. The essential aspect is the account of techniques Jinmu-Tennō, a descendant of Amaterasu, became the number one emperor of Japan. After which, the Kojiki dwells at the exploits of the successive rulers, attaining as a whole lot as the seventh century. The textual content is complicated, redundant, and hard to interpret. It is a tough but awesome starting for Japanese literature. It will acquire its top of refinement pleasant across the 12 months 1000 with that standard masterpiece, the Genji Monogatari, the flood novel via using Murasaki Shikibu.

The special super Japanese mythological textual content is the Nihongi. Later than the Kojiki, and polluted with the beneficial aid of heavy Chinese influences, the Nihongi evaluations the identical myths but with a few exciting variations.

Japanese mythology turn out to be born together with the philosophy, and primitive faith professed even earlier than the unfold of Shinto's Buddhist faith (truely method Way of the Gods). The dual term with which this religion have become to begin with alluded to is Kami-no or Doctrine of the Gods, in which Kami, a completely familiar term, represents the superhuman strength of people who stay each in Heaven and on Earth and of which there's a tremendous deal communicate in historical sacred texts.

The numerous classes:

Natural Kami (celestial and terrestrial)

Kami Cultural (community and functional)

Kami Umani (called Hitogami)

The celestial Kamis commonly represent heavenly our our our bodies or meteorological phenomena; the terrestrial embody physical and geological phenomena, plant life, and animals (imaginary and otherwise, along aspect dragons, foxes, and deer). Community kami defend a selected extended own family, at the equal time as purposeful kami deal with the approaches of human life, which encompass increase, professions, and the financial system. The human Kami as an opportunity are internal ancient characters identified as heroes or patriots.

The most well-known deities

Aizen-Myoo: is the deity of affection of prostitutes, feudal lords, singers, and musicians who had the power to soothe human passions and stimulate emotions of pity and altruism in the direction of others.

Gaki: They are described as hungry spirits who maintain the steadiness of the complete international. In Zen monasteries, it turned into everyday to make a small offering of meals to the gaki earlier than starting to devour.

Sambo kojin: is the Japanese god of cooking. According to the legends, it has faces and three pairs of hands "to eat better."

Jikininki: they're devouring corpses. They are the spirits of vain men and women whose greed averted their souls from mission eternal peace with the aid of the use of forcing them to live half of of a life through devouring corpses. A legend tells of a priest with a robust person named Muso Kokushi who someday modified into searching over the corpse of a person. Suddenly, a Jikininki came to eat that corpse with violence, but the priest's prayers freed the demon's soul, making him discover everlasting peace.

Kanbarinyudo is the god of bathrooms. He became invoked near the New Year, saying: "Kanbarinyudo hototogisu." With this prayer, one end up guarded in opposition to ugly encounters in moments of intimacy in the relaxation room.

Kiyo: Beautiful maid from Japanese legends. Kiyo worked in a tea room, and, in the destiny, a priest who used to transport there regularly fell in love together with her. After a few months, the priest won his ardour and averted further conferences, so Kiyo have been given very disappointed and sought revenge thru the magical arts: he changed right into a dragon and flew to the big monastery in which the priest lived. He observed it coming and concealed under the temple's bell, however the dragon, with a terrific jet of fireplace, melted the bell and killed the priest. The priest turn out to be punished badly due to the truth he have to no longer have allowed his preference to distract him from his primary obligation.

Chapter 11: The Origin Of The World

According to ancient Japanese legends, and extra exactly, within the 3 books of Kojiki (古事記, finished written in 712 AD), on the start of time, five powerful and historical beings appeared, the primary Kanji (神), each male and lady, every single and multiple, every well and evil, virtually, greater neutral than some thing else, superior to all our dreams and all our (and no longer best ours) yearning. These historical deities resided in Takama-ga-Hara (高天原). There are almost more than 8000 of them. Still, their significance is because of the reality they represent this kind of tiny detail of the human race that perhaps we've got were given were given by no means even considered, making us apprehend even extra the philosophical and cultural depth of the humans. Japanese.

It is uncertain whether or not or not or now not those beings can come what might also additionally "die of antique age, "but we recognize that seven generations of divinities succeeded those 5 primordial Kami, which ended with the brothers Izanagi and Izanami, who may be taken into consideration the number one man and primary woman.

Thanks to a legendary Naginata (an extended shaft weapon, very just like our halberds, however completing with a curved blade more like a sword than the weapon above), they created the world as we realise it. From the dust moved through this weapon prodigious, an island changed into born which can also later become Japan (and then shape the complete recognized international), which turns into their domestic. Izanami and Izanagi every have been brother and sister, however they decided that they needed to preserve on their lineage, and after figuring out to procreate, they commenced out out the ritual. According to a part of the as an opportunity male-ruled fable, the number one youngsters of the Kami were born hideous, deformed, and cruel due to the fact Izanami took the initiative in sexual sex. In assessment, at the identical time as the man or woman took it the second one time, the entirety went effortlessly.

What took place to the big children? According to three legends, they went to shape the terrible human beings of the Oni (鬼), the ruthless and big Japanese demons) hungry for meat, silly, and continuously sexually eager. The first eight youngsters of the 2 divinities were the 8 islands that might form Japan, and we out of place rely of the other youngsters. He got here after the union between Izanagi and Izanami, collectively with the primary human beings. However, it's miles stated that at a positive issue, Izanami died for the duration of childbirth, because the unborn infant have emerge as Kagu-Tsuchi, god of hearth, who burned his mom to lack of life along along with his flames. Poor Izanagi, livid, alongside along with his top notch Sword Tostuka-no-Tsurugi (十拳剣, absolutely, the Sword ten instances its hilt) reduce the brand new infant into 8 portions form the eight substantial volcanoes of Japan. From his blood, giant dragon deities had been born (consider the dragon, it is going to be a figure we are capable of almost constantly see) Watatsumi and Kuraokami, gods of the sea and rain, respectively.

Desperate Izanagi, he went to the terrible realm of the useless, the dark Yomi ((黄泉), to take her some distance from that worldwide of Darkness and pain, the kingdom of demons. And the Oni above (no matter the fact that they may be plenty extra powerful, they'll be in evaluation in strategies and intelligence to Western orcs, specifically those who got here after Tolkien's myth revolution).

Here, following the myth of Orpheus and Proserpina in an incredibly comparable manner, Izanami became cautioned that he must take her away from the Yomi as long as he did not observe her until they came out of that international of demise. Here, the author god determined that his cherished girl had eaten a few food from past the arena, which, as soon as ingested, does not permit each person as a way to go away the Underworld.

Izanagi, greatly surprised, decided that he would in all likelihood see her one extra time earlier than leaving at the back of her, and whilst she slept, he grew to turn out to be the flashlight toward her face; what he noticed plunged him into the maximum excruciating ache. Once beautiful, Izanagi, with prolonged black hair, pearl-white pores and pores and skin, and a narrow but bursting and seductive body, had turn out to be a massive being. Burned with the resource of flames and corrupted thru the forces of hell, his look have come to be now a good deal extra like a Yomi than a Kami. Izanami located out that she had been located and threw the mask; she had become the queen of that hideous worldwide, mom of every infernal being. Her husband, mad with worry, escaped from Yomi, however the fact that his ex-accomplice had thrown at him a fearsome lightning demon, a Raijin (雷神), who, as a power, can placed even a Kami-like Izanagi in severe problem. The demon queen, furious for her husband's "betrayal," promised him that she might possibly kill 1000 men every day;

Izanami, irritated, replied that he could create fifteen hundred a day. Thus, loss of life fell on our international, however it is also proper that constantly following a fantastic judgment that might not appear like it's miles profoundly nice; this is moreover the motive of why there are constantly extra childbirths than deaths within the worldwide. Even in recent times, they have got fun their Day of the Dead or Obon.

Today, Japan's feel of network, family, and death has modified substantially, and historic traditions have given way to greater Westernized questioning. With us, lack of lifestyles is visible as some thing impure, to be decorated, a topic that is first-rate not to speak about if not decorating it with mystifications and embellishes that fine serve to distract the mind and cloud the thoughts.

Death in Japanese mythology grow to be seemed as a few component inevitable, even as what subjects are the actions carried out in life. The pain of the shortage of existence of a loved one becomes a comforting feeling in case you take transport of as right with that his soul stays among us.

Izanagi preferred to wash off the filth that had blanketed him and done a purification rite lower decrease lower back on Earth. He dived proper right into a river and, blowing his nostril, gave rise to the god Susanoo (須佐之男), lord of hurricane and war; from his proper eye became born Tsukuyomi (ツクヨミ, 月讀), the deity of the Moon and from the left one Amaterasu (天照), goddess of the Sun.

THE JAPANESE KAGUTSUCHI DIVINITY (カグツチ)

Kagutsuchi is also known as Hinokagatsuchi, as said inside the Kojiki (the oldest modern-day chronicle in Japan, irrespective of the reality that it is able to be considered the Japanese Bible). At the same time, Homusubi-no-Mikoto is the call said in Nihon Shoki (after Kojiki). The call approach to shine, strength, and energy. He is the Kami of fireplace and protector of blacksmiths and potters. Let's in brief see the genesis of the primary Japanese Kami.

Japanese Kami, the deities

The genesis of the precept Japanese Kami

Kojiki become first translated proper away from the ancient Japanese language in 1938 through the Italian missionary Mario Marega. More presently, however, the interpretation have emerge as written thru Paolo Villani in 2006.

Izanagi and his accomplice and sister Izanami created all the deities, entrusting them with their role. Until Izanami generated the remaining Creator (Kagutsuchi) come to be critically burned, and shortly after, she disappeared, leaving Takama-ga-Hara (the residence of the Kami). This is some of the most critical and crucial occasions of Kojiki. The infection and next disappearance of Izanami started out the era of various Kami, collectively with Kanayamahiko-no-Kami (the

Goddess of Metals, born from Izanami's burn), Haniyasu-Hiko (the Kami of the Earth, taken from the last dejections of Izanami). In assessment, the closing Kami generated (born from the fluids of the kidneys) changed into the Kami of the Mizuhame-no-Mikoto Water.

Desperate and angry, Izanagi wielded the Ame-no-Ohabari (the Sword of Heaven) and killed Kagutsuchi, maintaining apart the frame of the hearth kami into eight elements from which the 8 fundamental Yama-no-Kami (protectors of the mountains) have been born.

THE KAMI PROTECTORS OF THE MOUNTAINS:

To-Yamatsumi (born from the top).

Masaka-Yamatsumi (taken from the chest).

Odo-Yamatsumi (taken from the womb).

Oku-Yamatsumi (taken of the reproductive gadget).

Kura-Yamatsumi (taken from the left hand).

Shigi-Yamatsumi (taken from the proper hand).

Ha-Yamatsumi (taken from the left foot).

Hara-Yamatsumi (taken from the proper foot).

While distinct very essential Yama-no-Kami are Ōyamatsumi (the elder brother of Amaterasu-ō-mi-Kami), the critical Kami who hints all of the mountains, protector of seafarers and infantrymen, and his daughter Konohananosakuya-hime (the Kami of the Fujisan).

THE DRAGON DIVINITIES

Iwasaku, the dragon deity of the Roots

Nesaku, the opportunity dragon deity of the Roots

Iwatsutsunō, the dragon deity of the Stone

Mikahayahi, the dragon deity of Speed

Hihayahi, the opposite dragon deity of Speed

Kuramitsuha, the dragon deity of Darkness

Kuraokami, the dragon deity of Rain and Snow

The dragon deity of the Sword (he is likewise considered the first Sumō fighter).

Izanagi later went to Yomi-No-Kuni in an attempt to get better his preferred. But the Underworld had infected Izanami via way of using transforming her, so disappointed Izanagi (as quickly as he escaped from the Underworld) through the ceremony of purification, he generated the 3 fundamental kami deities.

The firstborn Amaterasu-ō-mi-Kami, the girl Kami of the Sun (born of purification from the left eye), her 2d toddler, the male Kami of the Moon Tsukuyomi-no-Mikoto (taken of the proper eye), and in the end, the zero.33 born little one from the cleansing of the nostril Susanō-no-Mikoto, the Kami of Storms and the Sea.

SUSANOO, THE REBEL GOD

Susanoo, the youngest of the 3 noble youngsters (the 3 essential Kami born of Izanagi's purification ritual), his electricity and courage were matched exceptional through his audacity and warlike man or woman. Bored thru the monotony of the venture assigned to him (to defend the seas created through his father), he deserted him, giving himself to a chain of violent gestures towards people and other Kami. Furious along with his son, the father preferred to exile him from the takama-ga- Hara. Susanoo, earlier than leaving, however, had Izanagi's consent to move and notice Amaterasu earlier than leaving, the two after a trivial shaggy dog story or a guess received by way of the goddess of the Moon) went to fulfill a horrible quarrel wherein Susanoo killed all of the sister's maids and destroyed all of the cultivated fields. Amaterasu, shocked thru the violence of her extra younger brother, locked herself in a cave, plunging the region into Darkness. After having made her come out of the cave, way to a magic replicate, the moderate lower back to the arena. Izanagi nearly killed his son in anger and immediately chased him away, ordering him by no means to go lower back.

Having landed in the mortal international, Susanoo determined himself in the Izumo area, wherein he met three determined human beings: parents and a younger woman. The elders stated to him that a big being, a full-size eight-headed serpent, called Yamata no Orochi, who tyrannized over the peoples of that land, threatened to damage the whole thing inside the occasion that they did no longer provide him as a tribute virgins to devour. He had selected as his subsequent sufferer Kushinada, the younger daughter of the 2 elders.

Orochi, white like the Moon (White in Japan suggests everything indicated with the useful resource of black for us, Darkness and evil, and Orochi became one of the maximum effective incarnations. Even nowadays, within the land of the Rising Sun, it's far synonymous with cruelty and demise, and plenty of terrible characters from the area of anime talk to this discern. Above all, Orochimaru from Naruto and Frieza from Dragon Ball); he end up smelly and poisonous; their blood and breath may also need to instantly kill every creature. Susanoo, who, as speedy as he noticed Kushinada fell in love within the starting sight (feeling reciprocated), decided to help the human beings of Izumo, however he knew perfectly well that he could not face Orochi on my own; he become too sturdy, even for an indomitable and proud warrior like him. Susanoo then ordered 8 barrels of sake to be accrued and located in the the front of the residence in which the three lived. When Yamata no Orochi arrived in front of Kushinada's house, he discovered the 8 barrels of sake and couldn't help however get drunk until every head fell asleep. Only even as all the monster's heads fell proper right right into a deep sleep did Susanoo abandon his hiding region and reduce them off, the usage of the equal Sword that his father used to tear apart the fireplace god, killing the effective monster.

Soon after, Susanoo lessen Orochi's tails, but even as he reached the relevant bottom, he determined a few thing that stopped his Sword, certainly, even cracked it. Thus it changed into that Susanoo located the legendary Sword Ama no Murakumo. The blade become awesome and high-quality, so the Stormlord decided it'd be the right peacemaking present for his sister. He took her to Amaterasu, who, moved with the resource of the gesture, the adulthood received by means of the use of way of her brother, and the beauty of Murakumo, determined to forgive him, which Izanagi did too.

Susanoo, but, decided that the vicinity come to be now not the diverse Kami but alongside alongside with his cherished Kushinada, with whom he immediately married, in a promise of eternal love. Even in recent times, inside the Izumo vicinity, there may be a shrine reminding their passion.

AMATERASU, THE GODDESS OF THE SHINING SUN

Amaterasu, she who makes the skies shine; A top notch deity who lights up the sky, Amaterasu-O Mikami is the adorable and radiant Kami of the Sun.

Shinto deity, born in Japan spherical 500 BC, have grow to be joined with the aid of manner of Buddhism, coming from neighboring India.

Amaterasu modified into born from the left eye of Izanagi (the author god, father of all Kami), at the same time as his brother Tsukiyomi, god of the Moon, originated from the proper eye.

However, Izanagi moreover had a third little one, Susanoo, the god of the typhoon. Instead of bringing slight and serenity to the archipelago, Susanoo proved to be little inclined to speak and earthly peace. After a quarrel along with her sister Amaterasu, she destroyed all the rice fields and dams she created out of spite (in reality, mythology attributes the discovery of rice cultivation). Not content material, he barbarously skinned a pony and threw it on his loom (she is likewise credited with the use of the silkworm and the talent of weaving) after killing considered one in every of her assistants. These horrible gestures made Amaterasu shiver loads that out of disgrace, she took safe haven in a cave, plunging the Earth into limitless Darkness.

Thus starts the parable that the ancient Japanese defined the eclipse phenomenon: it modified into first recommended in Ise via way of some fishermen inside the area. The maximum crucial sanctuary committed to the goddess is positioned in Ise.

From this goddess originates the lineage of the Japanese royal family.

A well-known tale about Amaterasu tells that once a quarrel collectively together along with her violent brother Susano-o, the goddess concealed in a cave plunging the sector into Darkness. The special gods prepared a celebration out of doors the cave to entice her out. When Amaterasu, intrigued, went out to understand what modified into taking location, the gods located a shimenawa.

After the expulsion from Heaven and Amaterasu returns to gain men, coaching them rice cultivation, the breeding of silkworms, and the artwork of weaving. According to a few, this mythological motif symbolizes the sun eclipse. It is superb among many peoples of East Asia and is linked to shamanic rites from which the Kagura dances, one of the primitive forms of Japanese theater, drew their starting—beginning from the sec. IV, Amaterasu, progenitor deity of the imperial prolonged circle of relatives, obtained absolute pre-eminence over the gods of the opportunity households, turning into the superb deity in Japan.

Chapter 12: The Divine Origins Of The Emperors

Many years later, King Ame-no-Fuyu-gino, splendid-grandson of Susano-ō, reigned over the Izumo. He had the son Ō-Kuni-nushi from his first accomplice. He later had 80 different children through manner of numerous concubines.

In the kingdom of Inaba, east of Izumo lived a beautiful princess named Yagami. Each of the eighty brothers had determined to marry her, just so they left for Inaba to invite for her hand. Ō-Kuni-nushi located his stepbrothers as a servant, sporting the sack of provisions on his shoulders.

While taking walks alongside the seashores of Cape Keta, the 80 brothers got here within the route of a white bunny, absolutely bare because a crocodile had eaten his fur. Then the 80 brothers stated to him:

Bathe within the seawater, then go to the top of a mountain, in which the wind blows. So the fur will grow back.

The bunny did as he have become endorsed. He bathed inside the sea and then exposed himself due to the truth the wind blew. But as speedy due to the fact the water evaporated, the salt cracked his pores and skin, inflicting him splendid struggling. And lying on the seashore, the bunny was crying and despairing.

When the younger Ō-Kuni-nushi arrived and took pity on the animal, he stated to him: - Listen to me, bunny. Now wash in freshwater, then roll up on the red vegetation. You will see that your body will heal and soon regain the fur.

The bunny did due to the fact the younger guy suggested him and recovered.

Ō-Kuni-nushi

The story of Ō-Kuni-nushi and the Inaba rabbit is viral in Japan, as evidenced via a monument depicting the prince consoling the crying bunny. In the vicinity wherein the meeting ought to have taken region, the seaside of Cape Keta, nowadays, there can be an critical Shinto temple devoted to the god of the rabbit.

Meanwhile, within the kingdom of Inaba, Princess Yagami received the 80 brothers.

"We have come to ask you in marriage," they said to the princess. - Choose from us who may be your husband.

I have heard of your cruelty and your recklessness - she replied, Warned via the bunny - For this reason, I don't have any purpose of marrying any of you. The first-rate one that can aspire to my hand is your noble more youthful brother Ō-Kuni-nushi.

Out of jealousy, the 80 brothers conspired to kill Ō-Kuni-nushi. At first, they tried to burn him below a warm stone; then, they desired to overwhelm him with the resource of rolling a tree trunk on him. Ō-Kuni-nushi escaped each tries. But the 80 brothers gave him no respite and pursued him up the mountains, targeting him with arrows.

Then Ō-Kuni-nushi decided to head right all the way down to the Realm of the Deep to are trying to find recommendation from his ancestor Susano-ō.

Susano-ō lived inside the Deep corner of a large underground house. His lovely daughter Suseri changed into with him. Suseri have become standing on the doorstep at the identical time as Ō-Kuni-nushi arrived. The girl without delay fell in love with the younger man and determined that she would possibly have him as her husband.

But whilst Suseri brought Ō-Kuni-nushi inside the presence of Susano-ō, he stared at that descendant of his and decided to in my view check whether or no longer he emerge as as an awful lot as ascending the throne of Izumo.

Susano-ō ordered him to sleep in a cave complete of snakes. But Suseri handed Ō-Kuni-nushi a bandage and said: - When the snakes are about to chew you, shake the software program application three instances, and they'll go away. - Ō-Kuni-nushi did as he emerge as counseled and turned into capable of sleep peacefully.

Then Susano -ō sent Ō-Kuni-nushi to sleep in the cave of the poisonous centipedes. Still, once more Suseri intervened thru the usage of giving him a 2d magic bandage with which the boy also can want to searching for the centipedes.

Then Susano-ō shot an arrow inside the middle of a huge prairie and ordered Ō-Kuni-nushi to move and get it. And whilst the younger guy stood in the middle of the prairie, Susano-ō set fireside to the stubble from all instructions. Ō-Kuni-nushi decided himself all of sudden surrounded thru flames and have become glad that he may also want to die via burning even as a mouse came out of a hollow inside the ground and advised him to comply with him. Ō-Kuni-nushi located himself in an underground cave and became capable of live secure because the flames gobbled the prairie above him. When the entirety became burned, and Suseri changed into already mourning the dearth of Ō-Kuni-nushi, the young guy got here out of the prairie and held the arrow in his hand. Susano-ō commenced out, regardless of himself, to revel in admiration for his greater younger descendant.

Then Susano-ō ordered him to loose his hair from lice, which have been large and toxic. Suseri intervened yet again, giving Ō-Kuni-nushi a packet of berries, so the more youthful man, while rummaging via Susano-ō's hair, chewed the berries and spat them out. Susano-ō believed that the young guy changed into crushing his lice among his tooth and belief his descendant end up without a doubt really worth of him.

The operation persisted slowly, and Susano-ō fell asleep. Then Ō-Kuni-nushi undid his ancestor's hair and braided it to each beam in the room. Then he blocked the cave's door with a massive stone, carried Suseri on his shoulder, stole the god's Sword, bow with arrows, and harp embellished with pearls, and ran a long way from the Deep.

But at the run, the harp hit a tree and started out to play. Susano-ō woke up, understood what had took place, and at once jumped in pursuit of the younger man. But the hair stretched among the beams of the room, and through way of dint of pulling, Susano-ō introduced down the entire residence. The god had to waste valuable time untying all his hair, and within the period in-between, Ō-Kuni-nushi become coming out of the caves within the daytime.

When Susano-ō managed to extricate herself, she ran to the Deep part and, leaning out of the caves, saw the younger guy now an extended way away. Then he raised his voice and shouted after him:

Using the excellent Sword and bow you deliver with you, chase and bow down all your stepbrothers to the ends of the slopes, chase them and sweep them away within the rapids of rivers, and you, coward, turn out to be the lord of the whole Yamato! And can also moreover my daughter Suseri be your legitimate partner! Then, having reached the foot of Mount Uka, plant the columns of a building in the rock and lift the roof to the sky! And in that region, depressing, he lives and reigns!

Ō-Kuni-nushi did as his august ancestor Susano-ō recommended him. He worn out his half of of-brothers, married Suseri, erected a tremendous palace at the slopes of Mount Uka, and imposed his reign on Yamato. His second spouse have come to be Yagami, but he moreover had distinct better halves, and his offspring had been numerous.

ME-WAKA-HIKO COMES DOWN TO EARTH

Years exceeded, and inside the future, in the High Sky Plain, the goddess Amaterasu-ō-mi-kami have become her mind to the Earth and stated: - The land of the apparent of sufficient reeds, of one thousand autumns and 5 hundred prolonged autumns, it is the usa that my august eldest son will rule.

What emerge as called Masa-ka-a-katsu-kachi-haya-bi-ame-no-Oshi-ō-mimi-no-mikoto.

Oshi-ō-Mimi obeyed his mother's order and descended from Heaven to Earth. But right now after, Amaterasu noticed him skip returned terrified. - Mother! The land of Yamato is entire of fierce and sturdy demigods stirring relentlessly in order that the Earth trembles and resounds!

With an imperious command, Amaterasu gathered the 80 thousand deities at the dry mattress of the Milky Way River. Then he became to the assembly and stated:

The u . S . A . Of Yamato is the us that my august son Oshi-ō-Mimi will want to rule, which I truely have designed to provide to him and his descendants forever. Here, considering that on this u . S ., there are already the youngsters of Susano-ō-no-Mikoto, who are violent and whole of energy and power, what ought to we do to difficulty them to our will?

Omoi-Kane, the god of idea, spoke back: - Send noble Ame-waka-hiko to Earth. He will apprehend a manner to tame the proud soul of Susano-ō's descendants.

Then they passed the celestial bow to the more youthful Ame-waka-Hiko and ordered him to descend to Earth to subdue the descendants of Susano-ō. Ame-waka-hiko promised to ship commonplace reviews to tell the heavenly gods of her victories and fell from the sky, breaking thru the clouds.

But Yamato's country was so cute and welcoming that Ame-waka-Hiko determined he would possibly by no means cross decrease back to Heaven. He met with the king of the land, Ō-Kuni-nushi. But rather than transmitting Amaterasu's order to him, he married his daughter, Princess Shita-teru, and stayed with him as his son-in-law.

Thus 8 years exceeded, and Amaterasu and the heavenly gods waited in vain for Ame-waka-Hiko's report. Eventually, they sent a pheasant to Earth to look what happened.

The pheasant went all the manner all the way down to the land of Izumo, stopped on a tree that have become near the house of Ame-waka-Hiko, and started out out to name him in a noisy voice, asking him why he had no longer given in addition news of himself.

Annoyed by the decision, Ame-waka-Hiko brandished the bow and killed the pheasant. But after having pierced the animal, the arrow endured alongside facet its eating place, reached the sky, and stopped on the foot of Amaterasu. The goddess identified Ame-waka-Hiko's hand, then observed the blood on the tip and knew that the pheasant have been killed. Then he picked up the hand and stated:

If Ame-waka-Hiko has betrayed his home, permit this arrow kill him!

And he dropped the arrow to the Earth. Ame-waka-Hiko changed into napping in her house whilst the indicator fell whistling from the sky and planted itself in her chest. Thus the younger man died.

HANDSHAKES

A bizarre god inside the sky named Itsu-no-ō-ha-bari, who had barred the Milky Way River. His son, Take-mi-kazuchi, who grow to be of outstanding physical electricity, emerge as despatched to Earth with the challenge of conquering the united states of america on behalf of Amaterasu. With him went his partner, the god Ame-no-tori-bune.

The gods at once went to Ō-Kuni-nushi.

They stated to him: - The august remarkable goddess Amaterasu has despatched us to you. In this u . S . A . Of Yamato which you rule as a lord, you can have to give up to his son Oshi-ō-Mimi to reign for your region all of the time.

Ō-Kuni-nushi gave a wry smile. - Whoever comes to my united states and says such impiety deserves to revel in the strength of my son's palms.

www.ingramcontent.com/pod-product-compliance
Lightning Source LLC
Chambersburg PA
CBHW070556010526
44118CB00012B/1336